Germany

An Expat's Guide

German Expat Immigration, Housing and Living Options, Work & Business, Education, Marriage, Retirement, Taxes & Banking, Health Care, and Much More!

By Tess Downey

Foreword

Germany is one of the must – see countries in northern Europe because of its diverse culture and beautiful nation. There's something for every traveler and potential expats in Germany, with its ancient palaces, medieval - looking villages, glorious sceneries, amazing castles, and rich history, all within easy reach of the bustling towns and vibrant cities.

Take in all the spectacular sights and sounds of major cities like Berlin, Frankfurt, and Munich that offers everyone with a great taste of the German culture.

If you're thinking about relocating to Germany, you should prepare yourself for lots of fantastic experiences! From great dining and shopping places to the good times at various bars and night clubs, Germany will surely make you feel alive!

Explore the wonderful regions of the country and taste world – class food and wine, stroll through the cobble – stoned streets and half – wooded houses, breathe in the scenic view of the Bavarian Alps, tour the famous River Elbe, and be treated as one of them royals as you pass through the many ancient and majestic looking palaces and landmarks. Start anew and thirst your wanderlust as you socialize with the locals, visit famous sites, and discover hidden treasures of the country.

This book will provide you with plenty of information about how to settle in Germany as an expat, provide you with amazing opportunities you can take advantage of, and guide you to the beautiful places you can explore whether you're a young adventurer, a retired senior citizen, an exchange student, or someone looking to start and raise a family. This book will ensure your smooth relocation to one of the most significant countries in human history!

Table of Contents

Welcome to Deutschland! 1

Chapter One: An Overview of Germany.................................. 3

Quick Facts:.. 5

A Brief History of Germany 6

Germany At A Glance 13

Best Things to Do in Germany 14

Best Things to Eat in Germany.......................... 20

Climate and Seasons.. 25

Language and Religion 28

Social Norms, Etiquette and Customs 29

Clothing.. 30

Customs and Etiquette 31

Business Etiquettes 33

Chapter Two: Immigration Requirements 35

Visa vs. Residence Permit 37

90 Days Visa – Free/ Tourist Visa 38

The Residence Permit 39

Temporary Residence Permit 39

Permanent Residence Permit 40

Do I Need to Be Proficient or Fluent in German? 40

Residence Permit Categories 41

General Residence Permit Categories 43

German Citizenship 48

General Requirements 49

Chapter Three: Expat Hubs and Cost of Living in Germany

.... 55

The Expat Hubs in Germany 57

Cost of Living in Germany 69

Estimate Costs of Household Items in Germany 73

Chapter Four: Renting vs. Buying a House............................ 79

Renting in Germany 81

Common House Rules for Leasers 83

Finding Rent 86

Apartment/House Rental Terms... 87

Buying a House in Germany 90

Housing Costs 91

Buying an Apartment 95

How to Find and Buy a House or Apartment 95

Notary Duties and Responsibilities 99

The Contract 101

Financing Your House or Apartment 104

Mortgages 104

Chapter Five: Utilities and Communication Services in

Germany 107

Contracts and Payments 108

Gas/ Heating 108

Electricity 109

Water Supply 110

Telephone/ Internet Connections 111

Internet Providers and Basic Plans 113

Mobile Basic Plan Options 115

Relocation Services 118

Chapter Six: Work and Business in Germany 121

Finding a Job in Germany 122

Hiring Procedures and Employment Contract 123

The Employment Contract 127

Self – Employment in Germany 130

Free – Professionals/ Freelancers 133

Doing Business in Germany 136

Types of Business Structures 137

Sole Proprietorship 137

Limited Liability Company (GmBH - Gesellschaft mit

beschränkter Haftung) 138

Joint – Stock Company (AG – Aktiengesellschaft) 139

General Partnerships (OHG - Offene

Handelsgesellschaft) 140

Limited Partnerships (KG – Kommanditgesellschaft) 141

Limited Partnerships with a Limited Liability Company

as a General Partner (GmBH & Co KG) 141

Subsidiary (Töchtergesellschaft) 142

Branch (Zweigniederlassung) 142

Chapter Seven: Education System in Germany 143

Hauptschule (Grade 5 to Grade 9)..................................... 145

Realschule (Grade 5 to Grade 10) 146

Gymnasium.. 146

Gesamtschule (Comprehensive School) 147

Berufsschule 148

The School Day.. 149

The School Year 150

Schools for Students who have Special Needs 150

Private Schools 151

Internat (Boarding Schools) 151

International Schools 152

Parochial Schools 152

Home Schooling 152

Higher Education 153

Entrance Requirements 153

Chapter Eight: Taxes & Banking in Germany..................... 157

Individual Income Taxes.. 158

Other Taxes 162

German Tax Classes.. 163

Tax Returns for U.S. Citizens 166

State Taxes.. 167

General Requirements.................................. 167

Understanding FATCA as an American Living in
Germany 168

Additional Reporting Requirements........................ 171

Banks and Banking in Germany 172

Types of Banks.. 177

Payment Methods 177

Other Bank Services.. 179

Chapter Nine: Healthcare and Retirement in Germany..... 181

Public Insurance System 182

Government Health Insurance System (GKV) 182

Private Health Insurance (PKV)............................. 186

Retirement for Expats in Germany...................... 189

Retirement Contributions 190

Health Care for Retirees.................................... 191

Chapter Ten: Getting Married in Germany........................... 193

    Marriage Requirements... 194

        If one or both partners is a foreigner............................. 196

    Civil and Traditional Ceremonies 197

    Same - Sex Marriage 198

Relocation Tips 199

PHOTO REFERENCES 203

REFERENCES 211

Welcome to Deutschland!

Known for their efficiency and commitment, the Germans sure know how to create a country! A stunning combination of historical significance and futuristic drive, it is still one of Europe's powerhouse in the modern era. Any expat will surely enjoy the modern city life as well as the hidden treasures of the country. You'll get to explore romantic lanes, delicious national and international delicacies, historical museums, high – end shopping malls, cozy café bars among others that will surely make you crave for more! The towns and cities of Germany is filled with cultural events like no other; there are various conferences and trade fairs, operatic and theatrical plays, local and international concerts from world – class artists, open – air fests, city tours, sporting events and many more!

Any potential expats and tourist will surely get inspired by the power of Germany's capital, Berlin as well as the passionate vibe of Munich, and the festive culture of Germans all over the country.

You will soon find yourself as one of them Germans as you interact with the locals in various bars, restaurants, and flea markets. The mouth - watering German sausages and pretzels as you walk along the medieval villages and cobble – stoned streets will surely become part of your daily life!

The tragic past of the nation will make you feel as if you're part of history, and the future drive of the country will let you celebrate and be hopeful for what's to come. Often dubbed as the capital of Europe, Germany is definitely a country that any potential expat like you should consider.

Chapter One: An Overview of Germany

The name Germany came from the Latin word Germania. During the time of the Gallic War around 58 to 51 B.C.E., the Romans designated the term Germania to the people living in the eastern region of the Rhine. The area formerly known as Deutschland (Germania/ Germany) came from the root word *Volk* which means people. The Deutschland territory was ruled under the Roman Emperor or German king up until the 10th century. The locals retained the name of some of the older territories, and they designated it as the name of the federal states today; this includes Bavaria, Saxony, and Bradenburg among others.

Germany, officially known as the Federal Republic of Germany, is located in the north – central region of Europe, and shares boundaries with other countries including Poland, Austria, France, Denmark, the Netherlands, the Czech Republic, Luxembourg, Switzerland, and Belgium. As its official name suggests, the country is a confederation of 16 constituent states.

The population of the country is distributed in small to medium – sized local units but majority of the people lived in the western region or in West Germany. The cities with a population that's over a million are the following:

- Berlin (over 3 million)
- Hamburg (almost 2 million)
- Munich (more than 1 million)

Germany is considered one of the world's powerhouses. It is included in the top 5 largest economies, and it comes second as the most popular country for immigrants after the United States.

Quick Facts:

- **Capital:** Berlin
- **Main Language:** German
- **Main Cities:** Hamburg, Munich, Cologne
- **Major Rivers:** River Rhine, Elbe, Danube, Main
- **Main Currency:** Euro
- **Population:** 82.2 million
- **Size:** 357,168 sq. km
- **Major Religion:** Christianity
- **Climate:** Temperate seasonal climate
- **Life Expectancy:** 79 years (men), 83 years (women)
- **Standard Electricity Voltage:** 230 V; standard frequency is 50 Hz

A Brief History of Germany

We all know that Germany has played a very significant role in history especially during the 20th century; the World Wars surely put the country on the map, so to speak. Germany's tragic past definitely made the world a better place today. Let's look back at the most important events in the country's history as these events is what also helped shaped them to be the great powerhouse that they are today:

- 800: Pope Leo III, Emperor Charlemagne crowned Charlemagne as the Roman emperor and rule of Germany and France.

- 843: Germany became a separate territory due to the split of the Frankish Empire.

- 962: Otto I, King of Germany, took over Northern Italy and was crowned as the Roman Emperor. This was the beginning of the Holy Roman Empire that's centered on the Deutschland or Germany.

- 1250: The Holy Roman Empire collapsed after the death of Emperor Frederick II which led to the creation of independent territories.

- 1438: Albert I was elected and this began the Habsburg Dynasty in Austria.

- 1517: This is the time when Protestants led by Martin Luther split from the Catholic Church.

- 1618 to 1648: 30 Years War: The Habsburg emperor failed in their attempt to restore Catholicism as the dominant religion against the Protestants.

- 1806: Napoleon's army conquered Germany and becomes the emperor of Austria.

- 1813: Napoleon was defeated at the Battle of Leipzig.

- 1871: Otto von Bismarck unified Germany and subjected it under Prussia; the new Germany created an election for the national parliament but it still gives the emperor extensive powers.

- 1888: Beginning of William II's reign.

- 1890: The Social Democratic Party of Germany was founded.

- 1914 to 1918: World War I

- 1918: Germany was defeated, and Emperor William II abdicated and went on to be exiled.

- 1919: Treaty of Versailles; Start of the Weimar Republic. Germany lost its colonies to its enemies, and paid its dues. The early years of the new republic was marked by high inflation and unemployment.

- 1923: Adolf Hitler was at the time the leader of the National Socialist German Workers' Party (Nazi), and tries to create a coup in Munich.

- 1929: Worldwide recession and economic failure.

- 1933: The start of the Third Reich; Adolf Hitler becomes the chancellor. In 1934, Hitler officially proclaimed the Third Reich. The Jews were being persecuted.

- 1935: The German Jews was deprived of their citizenship based on the Nuremberg Laws.

- 1938: Jews are being attacked including their properties and synagogues.

- 1939 to 1945: World War II; the Nazis led by Hitler implemented an extermination policy to the Jews, Slavs, Gypsies and other races including homosexuals and religious dissenters.

- 1945: Germany and the Axis Powers were defeated by the Allies; Hitler commits suicide; the Allies divided the country into occupation zones.

- 1945 to 1946: Nazi figures were imprisoned and executed.

- 1949: The country was divided; the Soviet Zone in the eastern region became the communist German Democratic Republic while the western territories or the Allies' area became the Federal Republic of Germany.

- 1950's: The West Germany experiences a rapid economic growth.

- 1955: West Germany joins Nato while the eastern region joined the Warsaw Pact.

- 1961: The Berlin Wall was constructed to separate the West and the East.

- 1973: Both West and East Germany joins the United Nations.

- 1989: Germans in the east were able to go to West Germany as the Soviets loosen travel restrictions; the protests of East Germans led to the collapse of the Communist rule. The Berlin Wall was torn down by both the Western and Eastern Germans.

- 1990: The country finally merged and became a Federal Republic.

- 2005: History was made when Christian Democrat Angela Merkel becomes the first female chancellor after being elected in September of that year.

- 2008: Germany was officially declared in recession by November. In 2009, the country's economy grew and eventually recovered from the Financial Crisis.

- 2013 to 2017: Germany experienced the largest surge in immigration but the country eventually had a migrant crisis because of such surge.

- 2018: Chancellor Angela Merkel reforms the Grand Coalition with the Social Democrats.

Germany At A Glance

Before you learn the nuts and bolts of relocating to Germany, why not take a trip first so that you can see if this is the right country for you? This section will give you a glimpse of what kind of life you're going to have in this beautiful country. We highly recommend that you go on a trip for just a few days so that you'll have an idea about what Germany can offer to you or your family. We will share with you in this section some of the things that you need to experience as a traveller that pretty much sums up the real taste of what it's like to be one of them Germans.

Any potential expats should test the waters before taking the plunge, this way you can really have an overview of the country.

Best Things to Do in Germany

Visit the Great City of Berlin!

The first place you need to go to once you landed in Germany is the capital city of Berlin because this city pretty much sums up the kind of life you're going to have in the country once you finally make the move. Berlin is the largest and most populated city in the country, and most foreigners (both tourists and expats) flock in the capital because there are so many things to see and do, and perhaps because the city is the epitome of what it's like to be a true – blooded German. You'll definitely get a sense of what a German culture is like in general once you visited this place. In addition to its turbulent history, Berlin is home to many world – class museums, cheap gastronomic indulgences, arts and music culture, and vibrant night scene. The capital is also one of the most inexpensive cities that you can go to in Europe! Paris who?

Get Lost in Munich!

If you don't want to experience the crowded streets and the buzzing capital of Berlin, the next best city you can go to which also encompasses the German culture is Munich. The city is much less crowded than the capital but you can still get the feel of an authentic German experience. It is home to various historical museums, century – old establishments, plush parks, bars and cafes, trekking trails as well as local and international restaurants – not to mention the famous Oktoberfest that is being celebrated every year and attended by millions of tourists around the world! You will surely enjoy the sights and sounds of Munich and perhaps get to have more opportunity to interact with more locals than fellow foreigners.

Have the Time of Your Life in Oktoberfest!

Oktoberfest or Volksfest is the world's largest beer festival that's being held every year in Munich. Around 6 millions of people both locals and foreigners come here to celebrate and drink LOTS of pints of German beer while singing traditional German songs – there's nothing more German than that! The celebration lasts for around 18 days so better prep up your belly and see if you can survive this great beer festival! Cheers!

Explore other German Cities

Aside from Berlin and Munich, you can choose to visit other fantastic cities of Germany so that you can learn more about the German way of life. If you're the kind of person who loves nature, then Hamburg is a great place to visit since the city is famous for its spacious and plush parks as well as river canals. It also offers diversity and great German culture. If you tend to be more of a history buff, then Frankfurt should be included in one of your stops because it's home to many of the country's historical sights and even futuristic museums. Another great city to go to is Cologne; if you're more of an artsy person then this is the place to be! Soak yourself in the art scene and culture filled city.

Most foreigners who are thinking about relocating to Germany also visits Hanover; the city is underrated but if you want to get an authentic insight of the German culture and socialize with the locals then we highly recommend this place.

Experience the outdoors in Germany

If you're more of a nature lover, or you're someone who likes to stay away from the busy metropolis, then make sure to book a trip to the various natural landscapes in the country. Meet fellow outdoor enthusiasts, and soak yourself in the beauty of many lush forests, amazing trekking trails, and crystal clear lakes. We recommend that you go to Berchtesgaden National Park and just wander around there.

Another area that you can go to if you're an outdoor enthusiast is the famous Black Forest. This is the setting of the Grimm Brothers fairy tales! It borders France and the place is widely known for its dense forests, enchanting villages, and lots of hiking trails. Stumble upon many charming Gothic buildings and vineyards as well as breathtaking views.

Best Things to Eat in Germany

After getting a sense of the sights and sounds of various German cities, the next thing you need to consider is to get a taste of the German life through the country's various cuisines and gastronomic indulgences.

There is more to German cuisine than meat! The country is often outshined by other European cuisines like Italian, Spanish, and French but I assure you, the food of

Germany is just as delicious as the cuisines of its neighboring countries. It's both hearty and traditional, and definitely a must – try for tourists, especially for potential expats like you.

Here are famous and traditional German dishes you should try:

Bratwürste

If there's one meat that most Germans love to eat, it is this! Every local and foreigner knows and loves the classic Bratwürste sausage! You can feast on this delicious meat deli wherever you are in Germany though the locals recommend eating the best Bratwürste sausages from a place called

Nürnberg. You have not come to Germany if you haven't tasted this sausage.

Spätzle

This dish is one of the most famous pasta (and vegetarian) dish in the country! I told you they're not just all meat! It's a pasta dish that consists of eggs, cheese, flour salt, and a splash of fizzy water that fluffs up the dough. If you're a vegetarian, this is definitely a must – try.

Maultaschen

Another must – try pasta and meat dish from Germany is the Maultaschen. It's a ravioli dish that's packed with spinach, minced meat, and sauerkraut. You can eat them fried or boiled but either way, it's heaven on a plate!

Brezel

Last but definitely not least is Germany's version of New York's cronut (crossover of croissant and donut) called Brezel. It's a German pretzel that's mouth – watering and truly a must – try in the country. The Brezel is twisted into a bracelet shape brown crusted pretzel with a glossy and crisp dough on the inside. Fortunately, you can taste and devour on these awesome food almost anywhere in the country!

Visiting cultural places in Germany, interacting with the locals through various activities, and trying out the German cuisine will already give you a glimpse of what's like to be one of them Germans. If you find that you had a great experience in your mini – trip, then perhaps relocating in Germany might be ideal for you.

Climate and Seasons

Germany typically has a moderate climate with only a few extreme and unpredictable weathers throughout the year. The country has 4 seasons:

- Spring: From March to May

- Summer: From June to August

- Autumn: From September to November

- Winter: December to January

January is the coldest month of the year during the winter season; the average temperature is between 20 and 3 degrees Celsius depending on the area of residence. On the other hand, July is the warmest month in summertime, with temperatures ranging from 16 to 30 degrees Celsius.

Rain is very likely to happen throughout the year, and often in unpredictable times. Heavy snowfall also occurs during winter.

The most humid month is December while the least humid month is May. Humidity levels in the country range around 60 to 80%. Germany is a country that's filled with lush forests and green spaces that are very suitable for farmers because of the varying climate and consistent rainfall.

Obviously, you would need to pack up warm clothing like sweaters and coats especially around winter time. During summer months, you can just wear more lightweight clothing, and you may not need to wear a jacket because it'll be quite humid. Make sure to also pack a raincoat or any waterproof clothing especially during rainy days.

It's ideal that you make the move around summertime up until autumn (May to September) since the weather is warm and pleasant though rainfall could still occur every now and then so be prepared.

Weather – wise, Germany is safe from extreme weather conditions. The only main threats are occasional heavy storms that could bring hail, heavy rain, lightning, and strong winds from time to time. Be aware of the so – called föhn winds because it usually brings illnesses such as coughs and colds.

Language and Religion

The official language of the country is German. It originated from the West Germanic family of languages that's also spoken in other countries like Austria, Switzerland, Belgium, the Netherlands, and Luxembourg. The German language has been highly influenced by other languages like French and English. Lately, more and more English words are being included in the German language which is why some people refer to it as "Denglisch."

When it comes to religion, most Germans are Christians. Two - thirds of the population is Protestants, and about one – third is Roman Catholics. Germany is where the protestant reformation originated which is a major schism from the Catholic Church. Protestantism is becoming a popular religion in Germany.

Social Norms, Etiquette and Customs

     The culture of Germany was shaped through the prevalent cultures within the European continent. It is also defined within the states of which it's formed. Germany originated from the Germanic tribes that inhabited the region of Rhine during the ancient times. It eventually became part of the Holy Roman Empire. The Germany we now know today was first established in 1871 when the constituent states were unified into one country under the leadership of Prussia.

The country also played a major role with regards to the spread of Christianity throughout the West. Germany was also home to some of the most notable artists, writers, poets, philosophers, scientists, and musicians in the history of Western Civilization including Nietzsche, Beethoven, Kant, Rubens, Handel, Goethe, Bach, the Grimm Brothers to name a few.

This section will give you an overview about the German culture, norms, and etiquettes so that you can better interact with the people once you finally make the move.

Clothing

Germans dress up like a typical Westerner. In a business context, the typical clothing worn by men is the classic dark suit with ties or shirts, while women wore a good old' dress or a skirt paired with blouse.

The country does have a rich heritage of traditional clothing that varies significantly throughout the different areas within the country. Perhaps the most well – known traditional German costumes are those that are worn by locals in the state of Bavaria particularly during traditional

German festivals like the Oktoberfest. The costume includes Lederhosen which are leather trousers that has a length above the knee (usually brown in color) and is quite similar to a jumper; it's also paired with white long sleeve polo and a traditional Bavarian hat. For women, the traditional dress called the Dimdl has a blouse, bodice, apron and a full skirt.

Customs and Etiquette

One of the main principles of Germans is organization. They pride themselves for being highly organized people both in their personal and professional lives, and are culturally known for striking the balance between the two. This is why respecting the rules and regulations are very important especially if you're planning to live here for good.

<u>Jay – Walking Alert!</u>

Usually foreigners are caught off guard with regards to jay – walking. Many tourists often get fined on the spot since German authorities are very strict in enforcing laws when it comes to crossing the road that's not in the designated pedestrian crossing.

Privacy is Important

Professional and personal lives for the Germans should be separate. Therefore, if ever you got invited to a social gathering or over dinner with your colleagues, it's not an appropriate time to discuss work – related issues or continue discussing business – related matters; in fact if you do, it could be disrespectful for some. Germans are quite private people especially when it comes to their household. You shouldn't bring up family issues or concerns in the workplace, and don't be alarmed if you're not invited to come over to someone's home especially if you mean business.

Punctuality Goes a Long Way

If ever you get invited over for a social gathering, then make sure that you arrive on time. Punctuality for the Germans means that you are respectful, and also a highly – organized individual. You should also bring a small gift like wine, chocolates, or flowers (depends on the occasion) whenever you get invited. Expect that the gift you give will be opened or consumed right away.

Business Etiquettes

When you're meeting Germans for business purposes, the greeting or introduction is usually short with a firm handshake. Try to maintain eye contact whenever you're talking to someone but of course don't stare too long otherwise your business acquaintance will get uncomfortable.

Germans take pride in their titles and/or qualifications so make sure that if you're meeting someone who has a title (ex: doctor, professor, degree – holder etc.), you address them as such to show respect. If you plan on giving your business card, Germans are usually impressed whenever anyone has a title after their name.

When it comes to business meetings, you should make sure to plan and inform them ahead of time so that your colleague or business partner will have time to prepare for it schedule wise. When you arrive for a business meeting, make sure that you start right away.

It's also important to note that being way early is just as a misstep as being late because for the Germans, it shows poor planning on your part, so try not to arrive way too early before the scheduled time.

Germans are also decisive individuals but before they close any deal, they want to first analyze thoroughly the information given to them. If you're going to pitch or propose any business ideas, make sure that you provide them with lots of information and prepare to justify the points you want to make. Try not to rush people or push people to make a decision right away, give them time so that they won't see you as someone who are aggressive or even disrespectful. Avoid making any sudden changes in your plans whether it's for personal or business purposes because Germans don't like that; it will make you look unorganized, and they would likely not trust you when it comes to handling details.

Chapter Two: Immigration Requirements

There are usually different rules for those who are European citizens, and those that are foreign nationals coming from outside Europe. The information in this chapter is primarily aimed for citizens living in North America but it also applies for immigrants coming from Asia, Australia, Middle East, and other parts of the world. If you want to learn more about the exemptions and other specific laws for each country concerning entry/ permanent residency to the Federal Republic of Germany, we recommend that you inquire at the German Embassy in your home country or visit the website of the German Foreign Office at

<https://www.auswaertiges-amt.de/en >.

If you wish to live, study, or work in Germany for a period of time, or for good then it's a must that you apply for a visa along with other permits. This chapter will guide you in finding out how to get a German Residence Permit and choose the best option for you depending on your current status and nationality.

Applying for immigration is one of the very first steps you need to do before even planning where you're going to stay or researching about other expat essentials. The processing of papers and filing of documents that are needed for you to make a smooth transition will definitely take quite a period of time, energy, and money which is why this is a very crucial step. Once you're approved and ready to go, everything will be quite easier. You would want to make sure that everything is approved and documented properly so as not to have the possibility of being deported or have problems down the road once you've completely moved in.

Visa vs. Residence Permit

Many people confuse a residence permit as already being a travel visa. It doesn't mean that once you already got a German visa, you are already an immigrant, or you already have a permit to stay in the country for more than the allowed duration period. Your German visa once approved will only allow you to stay in the country for around 3 months (90 days). Canadians and Americans are allowed to go to Germany as a tourist (still within 3 months) without any German visa.

A Resident Permit requires a travel visa/ German visa but once approve, the document allows you to stay in the country as an immigrant (beyond the 90 – day rule). This is what you're going to learn in the next few sections.

90 Days Visa – Free/ Tourist Visa

Citizens from North America and other continents aforementioned can come to Germany as a tourist before they can apply for a residence permit. As a matter of fact, this is what most immigrants do. Citizens from non – EU/ EEA countries also apply for a residence permit before they arrive in the country. Even if you can get a travel visa and be able to come to the country as a tourist for 90 days, it is better that you already start the application process for your residence permit once you've already decided to relocate to the country so that you can already prepare ahead of time since it will involve lots of filing and acquiring of needed documents on your part.

The Residence Permit

A German Residence Permit (*Aufenthaltserlaubnis*) grants any foreign nationals to become a resident of Germany beyond the non – visa tourist limit. Back then, residence permits are called as residence visa this was during the time when a residence visa is either pasted on a passport page, or was written down on a separate document. For the entire chapter, we will use the term residence permit to avoid confusing it with a travel visa.

The residence permit today is an eAT document that comes in the form of a plastic card with a digital chip on it. This will allow any foreign national or potential expats like you to legally reside and stay in Germany. There are 2 types of residence permit, they are as follows:

Temporary Residence Permit

This is only valid for a certain period of time (months/ years), and it should be periodically renewed.

Permanent Residence Permit

Also known as the Settlement Permit, this is similar to a "Green Card" in the United States which allows a foreign national to permanently reside in the country as if he/she is a German citizen but it only grants legal residence not German citizenship. If you wish to be a German citizen and be treated as a first – class citizen/get all the government benefits, you will need to follow a different set of rules which we will talk about later; having a permanent residence permit though is the pre – requisite if you're planning to become a German citizen.

Do I Need to Be Proficient or Fluent in German?

Any aspiring expat or foreign national is not required to be fluent in the German language but you need to pass a proficiency language test otherwise you may not get a long – term residence permit. We highly recommend that you start learning the national language as soon as possible if you're serious about relocating to the country. You will also enjoy your expat experience in Germany if you know how to communicate using their language. It'll be an advantage for you to learn the basic as it will come in handy during your interview with the German consulates. Sometimes, you may be required to attend a language school in Germany and be given a conditional permit for a limited time (a few months up to a year) but it can't be extended. You will likely be granted a residence permit if you have the basic language skill.

Residence Permit Categories

Whether you're planning to work in the country or not, you will need to get the appropriate residence permit depending on your status and purpose. Back in the day, the residence permit and the working permit are not separated but due to the influx of immigrants to Germany, the government created categories that each has its own limitations and duration period that would be suited for any category whether you're a student, an accompanying spouse/ family member, a retiree, freelancer/ employee, artist, etc.

If you acquired a residence permit stating that you can't work, then that means it is illegal for you to engage into any employment activities. So make sure to plan ahead and take the time to know the rules of immigration so that you'll know what type of residence permit best suits you before you apply for it, and also avoid violating any immigration laws. There are four basic categories of residence permits issued by German authorities:

- **Residence permit:** This is a limited - time residence title; with or without employment).

- **EU Blue Card:** This is a limited-time residence title; highly qualified (for nationals whose countries are member of the European Union).

- **Settlement permit:** This is a permanent residence title.

- **EU permit for permanent residence:** This is a permanent residence title (for nationals whose countries are member of the European Union).

Any German residence permit that's being issued to a foreign national is based on the compliance of various conditions and requirements. Settlement permits are usually granted after a foreign national has lived in the country for a minimum of 5 years. There are expats who have been residing in the country for 5 years or more but still aren't granted a settlement permit which is why they need to renew their limited – term permit/ residence permit every 2 to 3 years. If you wish to be granted with a settlement permit, the German authorities will require that the applicant has a high level of German language proficiency.

General Residence Permit Categories

Even if there's no separate working permit for expatriates looking to find a job in Germany, you may still be able to legally work provided that there is a statement on your residence permit that allows you to do so. There are different categories of residence permits that will allow you to legally work in the country whether you're planning to work as an employee or start your own business. Regardless if you're going to work or not, you must show to the

German authorities upon your application that you have a sufficient amount of funds (either from your retirement, savings, pension, or investments) to live in the country without becoming a burden to the state.

It's important to note that the permit categories listed below each has its own limitations and special conditions which are related to the requirement of the state/ foreign affairs department; this includes the required documents, health insurance, language proficiency, funds, length of stay, purpose etc. Check out the categories below:

- **Section 16: Education, School, and Studies:** This is a residence permit category that's suitable for foreigners who wish to study in the country at the undergraduate or graduate level. An aspiring student expat may also be granted with a special German – language study visa (usually valid for 3 months to a year but cannot be extended) which would require you attend a language school in the country.

- **Student Applicant:** This residence permit is only for expat students who haven't been accepted yet by a German school or educational institution.

- **Section 21: Freelance/ Self – Employment:** The residence permit issued is only valid for up to 3 years though it can be extended under certain circumstances. This permit covers entrepreneurs, artists, teachers, architects, musicians, and jobs that are in the freelance field.

- **Section 20: Research:** This is given to those who need to conduct a research study in the country that's tied up to a specific university or research institution. It's only valid for around 1 year.

- **Section 17: Vocational Training or Internship:** This is valid for those who will stay in the country for the purpose of internship or a training course. The permit can be extended for a year to be given a chance to find employment.

- **Section 19a: European Union Blue Card:** This is only issued for those who are university graduates and highly qualified individuals. It will require a minimum annual salary of 50,800 Euros. It's only valid for the term of the employment and can be renewed for a maximum of 4 years. This also includes bringing of family members, and it can also be converted into an unlimited settlement permit under certain conditions.

- **Section 18: Skilled Employment:** This is quite similar to the EU Blue Card, and this is usually hard for North Americans to acquire as it involves trade skills and not just a white – collar type of employment. If you are a non – EU citizen, a company wishing to hire you should prove to the German government that no one else in the country or in the European Union has the capability to do the job. Usually, expats acquire this type of visa through the employer/ firm that hired them and wants them to be transferred to Germany for work purposes. The permit is only valid for the term of employment.

- **Section 18c: Job Search:** This allows an expat to stay in the country for just 6 months if he/ she wish to find employment.

- **Sections 28 and 29: Family Reunification: This involves any spouse, underage child/children, and parents). This is aimed** for family member who wish to enter the country in order to be united with a family that's already residing in Germany. Expats that used this category are those who are married to a German citizen or planning to marry a German citizen. The residence permit is valid for 3 to 5 years and can also be renewed.

- **Section 9: Settlement Permit:** This is the unlimited permanent residence permit that any immigrant wants. This is only granted to foreign nationals who have stayed in the country for a minimum of 5 years though they are still subjected to certain conditions. Aside from language proficiency, certain documents are strictly required before one can be issued with this status.

- **SoFA (Status of Forces Agreement):** This is for military personnel of the United States, and government officials including their families who wish to reside in Germany. It is subjected under special conditions between the U.S. and Germany (NATO member).

German Citizenship (Deutsche Staatsbürgerschaft)

If you want to eventually acquire a German citizenship, a residence permit might help in your application but you will still need to meet certain requirements. The general requirements are as follows:

- Must be a resident of Germany for a minimum of 5 years
- Must be proficient in the German language
- Must pass the Citizenship Test

The requirements and the laws are all subject to change so make sure to inquire first at the German Embassy in your home country or visit the official website of immigration at www.bamf.de/EN/Migration/migration-node.html for updates.

General Requirements

Before you go and submit your application to the Aliens Authority (Auslanderbehorde), you will need to first take care of very important documents and follow a certain processing procedure. If you do not produce complete documents such as the general requirements listed below, you will be rejected until all the requirements are met. Here are some of the things you need to accomplish in addition to other specific instructions/ conditions that the German consulate will ask from you:

Requirement #1: Registration Document (Anmeldung)

All citizens and immigrants that are residing in Germany are required to register their place of residence with the local authorities in each state. Since you're planning to become an expat and stay in the country for more than 90 days, you will be required to register your home address. The same process applies if you decide to one day move from one state to another, you'll have to de – register your address. In addition to the certificate of registration, the foreign affairs office may also need a proof of residence such as home ownership title or if you're renting, a copy of the lease.

Keep in mind that this is one of the first things you need to do so make sure to take care of this legal requirement as soon as you already bought/ rented a place to stay in the country. If you don't have a registration document, you won't be able to apply for a German bank account.

Requirement #2: Bank Account (Bankkonto)

Any expat or foreign national who is applying for a residence permit must be able to show the German authorities that they have sufficient funds or income sources. You can prove that you have the capability to support yourself through your bank statements or other paper assets that demonstrates your financial resources. You will need to also register for a German bank account since having a debit/ credit card is also a necessity in the country for everyday transactions. Keep in mind though, that if you plan on getting a German credit card, it's not like how a typical credit card works; for instance, if you charge a purchase for 100 Euros, what happens is that your bank will automatically deduct that debt from your account on your next card statement, which means that you won't have an option in paying it off via installments like how it is done in most countries (more on this later in the banking chapter). This is because Germans do not like debt.

Requirement #3: Health Insurance (Krankenkasse)

German citizens including foreign nationals are required to have a health insurance. Immigrants or those who have a long – term residence permit needs to have health insurance coverage from a local insurance company because other policies made in other countries will not be valid; this includes North American citizens. There are two types of health insurance; public and private. If you're not yet sure what plan will best suit you, what you can do is to just get a 1 year policy from a private insurer and see if it is the right option (more on this later in the Health Care chapter of the book).

Requirement #4: German Language Proficiency (Sprachkenntnisse)

As mentioned earlier, authorities will require any aspiring residents to learn and achieve a level of German language proficiency because this will further help an expat to become integrated to the German way of life. Your residency application will go smoother if you can speak and understand at least the basic though it's not yet required once you have initially applied. This is why we highly recommend that you take the time to learn some German words while you're still preparing for your application.

If you wish to acquire a permanent settlement permit, or perhaps plan on acquiring citizenship in the future, then you will be required to prove that you are learning the language, and be able to demonstrate high – levels of German language proficiency particularly during interviews. German language skills have levels that determine how proficient you already are. The Council of Europe created a set of language standards consisting of 6 levels of proficiency. It is used not just in Germany but also in other countries that are members of the European Union – this is called the Common European Framework of Reference for Languages (CEFR).

German authorities will assess an applicant's language proficiency using the CEFR (GER - Gemeinsamer Europäischer Referenzrahmen für Sprachen) standards. The levels range from A to C with level A being the starter's stage, and level C being the highest or most proficient stage. Each levels are also divided into 2 sub – levels, they are as follows:

- Level A1
- Level A2
- Level B1
- Level B2
- Level C1
- Level C2

Foreign nationals usually need to at least achieve a Level B2 proficiency of the CEFR so that one can have no problems when applying for a residence permit. The general guidelines for a Level B2 proficiency are as follows:

- Able to understand the main points of clear standard input on matters that are regularly encountered in everyday life such as in the workplace, school, leisure activities, other engagements etc.

- Able to deal with situations that is likely to arise while one is travelling to a place where the German language is spoken.

- Able to produce simple connected texts on topics that are of personal interest.

- Able to describe goals, events, stories, experiences, and can also provide explanations for certain opinions/ plans.

Chapter Three: Expat Hubs and Cost of Living in Germany

With the country's strong economy and high quality of life, it's no wonder that Germany is one of the top choices for expats who are looking to relocate and find work. Germany is one of the top 5 of the largest economies in the world based from the International Monetary Fund but with so many great cities to choose from, it can be quite difficult to decide on where exactly would you or your family wants to settle in in the country. You can also asks your fellow relatives and friends who are already living in Germany, or check out different expat forums online so that you can have an idea if a certain area can give you plenty of work or business opportunities. Before deciding where to rent or buy a house, make sure to explore and do some due diligence so that you can ensure that you'll get the best possible German living experience.

There are many factors to consider when choosing the best place for relocation so make sure to weigh the pros and cons of each as it could directly affect both your professional and personal life.

To help you find the best city for you and your family, this chapter will provide you with an overview of the top places in Germany where expatriates commonly live.

Chapter Three: Expat Hubs and Cost of Living in Germany

The Expat Hubs in Germany

Expat Hub #1: Berlin

The German capital is situated directly on the River Spree and the country's seat of government. Many expats say that Berlin is more diverse than New York City! This is because it's a multi – cultural place that comes with a glamorous lifestyle from culture, architecture, night life, business, and the arts. The city of Berlin is also known as the startup capital of Europe and it's also home to world –

renowned companies including Volkswagen, SAP, Pfizer which is why the city is perfect for foreign nationals seeking for employment in the field of business, science, arts, and technology.

Berlin is among the top 10 capitals in the world. The city boasts various high – end shopping malls, world – class restaurants and it is also rapidly becoming a center of fashion and the arts. The world is changing fast, and Berlin is a city that will take you to the front seat!

Expat Hub #2: Frankfurt

The next top hub of expats in Germany is the city of Frankfurt. It is the country's 5th largest city, and also a center of commerce and education. It is home to the headquarters of the European Central Bank, Deutsche Bank, German Federal Bank, and the Frankfurt Stock Exchange.

Frankfurt is the financial district of Germany which is why it's a perfect place for foreign nationals looking to start a career in banking and finance. There are an estimated of 800,000 residents living in Frankfurt but it's not as crowded as the capital, which makes it an ideal choice for expats who

prefer to live in a smaller and perhaps less "loud" city.

Expat Hub #3: Munich

Munich is the 3rd largest city in Germany with a

population of more than a million residents. It is known as

the cultural center of Germany, and it's also home to global

corporations including Siemns, MunichRe, BMS, Allianz,

Linde, and MAN.

About 38% of the city's population consists of expats from around the world, making it very appealing for those who wanted to experience the German culture with fellow foreign nationals.

If you choose to stay in Munich, you'll have a VIP access to the famous festival in the country – the Oktoberfest!

Expat Hub #4: Leipzig

Also known as Hypezig, Leipzig is becoming more and more popular for expats wishing to reside permanently in the country. The city is home to famous car companies like Porsche and BMW as well as famous classical musicians like Wagner, Mendelssohn, and Bach. Expats can enjoy the cultural and art scene in this awesome city.

Expat Hub #5: Stuttgart

Stuttgart has a young tech savvy population, and it's also the center for high – tech industry jobs because it is home to many research, academic, and scientific organizations. You'll meet fellow inventors and scientists

here! No other place in Germany registers as many patents
as Stuttgart does!

Expat Hub #6: Cologne

Cologne is the 4th largest city in Germany with a
population of over a million residents. It is located on the
famous Rhine River, and it's a city filled with historical sites
and spectacular medieval architecture. It is the center of
media and creative arts perfect for expats who have a
creative background. This is the Hollywood of Germany!

The city is home to various national TV stations though you will also see branches of major corporations like Ford and Lufthansa.

Expat Hub #7: Hamburg

Hamburg is the 2nd largest city, next to Berlin. It has a population of about 1.8 million residents, and also a popular tourist spot in the country. It is home to many professional sporting teams and banks in Germany. In addition to that,

Hamburg is the 3rd largest port in Europe, making it a source

of various work related in logistics.

Expat Hub #8: Bremen

Bremen is a small city with only around 550,000

residents. The city offers many blue – collar jobs particularly

jobs that are related in engineering and machineries. It is

home to Mercedes and Airbus factories, and this is where

most skilled laborers from around the world reside. Bremen

also boasts many beer breweries including the famous

Beck's and St. Pauli Girl.

Expat Hub #9: Dortmund

Dortmund was once famous for being the center of
the coal and steel industries. Today, the city has shifted to a
much more high – tech industry particularly in the field of
robotics, biomedical technology, and micro – systems
technology. It's a great option if you're seeking for a chance
to work in technology – related fields since there are lots of

high – tech jobs you can find. Dortmund is also known as Technologiepark Dortmund or a technology hub of the country.

Expat Hub #10: Dresden

Dresden which is located in the Saxony region is like the Silicon Valley of Germany which is why it's often referred to as "Silicon Saxony." Its economy is dominated by the tech industry, and many expats also live here because it has excellent levels of accessibility, innovation, education, and diversity. The Hamburg Institute of International Economics ranked Dresden as the 4th best city for future growth.

Here are other cities in the country that expats consider to reside in mainly because of employment opportunities:

- Aachen
- Nuremberg
- Darmstadt
- Bielefeld
- Hagan
- Heidelberg
- Karlsruhe
- Erlangen
- Hof
- Jena

Cost of Living in Germany

Just like in any other countries, the cost of living in major urban cities are generally higher but the upside is that there are more work opportunities which can hopefully maximize your wage, and offset the high living costs through a high paying job.

Accommodation

The largest part of your expenses and the most essential of necessities is your accommodation. Housing

costs will depend on where you will choose to reside in the
country, and what your housing standard will be. Many
expats in Germany especially those living in urban areas
rent apartments since buying a house in metropolitan areas
are very expensive. The most expensive rental
accommodation in Germany is Munich followed by
Frankfurt, Hamburg, Stuttgart, Cologne, Berlin in no
particular order.

Groceries, Restaurants, and Utility Costs

Standard groceries are generally inexpensive
compared to other European countries, but of course this
will again depend on your budget, and on how much food
you will consume in a month.

Restaurant and fast food meals costs lower than U.K.
and the U.S., quality is also higher. 10% tip is the usual
norm.

When it comes to utility costs, it's relatively expensive
(due to fluctuating prices of electric resources decided upon

Chapter Three: Expat Hubs and Cost of Living
in Germany

by the German government, but again it will also depend on your daily consumption.

Public Transportation

Public transportation in the country is of average cost compared to other European countries. If you are thinking about getting a car, it's relatively expensive compared to other countries in Europe mainly due to the cost of maintenance and car insurance.

Conclusion

We will tackle more about the expenses of your basic necessities in the next chapter, but you can still check out the next section if you want to gauge the costs for such necessities.

Keep in mind that your cost of living will depend on your individual lifestyle and daily consumption. You can save on accommodation by renting, and save your income by just getting by using the public transportation (especially if you're living in an urban area). You can purchase low cost grocery items at discount supermarkets, and eat out less if you're really tight on budget. Clothes can be as inexpensive as you want them to be. It will all be up to you on how to live within your means.

A single person making about 2,000 €/ month (net income) can definitely afford a comfortable life in Germany.

Estimate Costs of Household Items in Germany

This section will give you a breakdown of the cost of basic necessities in Germany on average. Depending on the region or city you choose to settle in, it's essential that you know how much your day to day expenses will be before you decide to move. The currency is in Euros (€), so just convert these items in your national currency so you can have a gauge at the costs of each. The prices of the items below are subject to change.

Restaurants/ Bars/ Market	Average Cost (Euros)
Three – course meal for 2; mid – range restaurant	45 €
Fast Food Combo Meal	7 €
Domestic Beer	3.50 €
Imported Beer	3.00 €
Cappuccino	2.65 €
Coke bottle	2.20 €
Water bottle	1.81 €
Bread (good for 1 day)	1.23 €
1 litter of Milk	0.71 €
1 kg of Rice	2.04€
12 Eggs	1.64 €
1 kg of Cheese	8.93 €
1 kg of Chicken Breasts	7.45 €
1 kg of Beef	11. 60 €
1 kg of Apples	2. 23 €

1 kg of Tomato	2.60 €
1 head of Lettuce	0.88 €
Cigarettes (20 pack)	6.30 €

Clothes	Average Cost (Euros)
1 pair of jeans (branded)	75. 85 €
1 dress/ top dress (branded)	32.50 €
1 pair of rubber shoes (branded)	83 €
1 pair of leather shoes (branded)	103. 50 €

Transportation/ Commute	Average Cost (Euros)
1 liter of gas	1.36 €
Ticket for public transportation (one way local transport)	2. 75 €

Personal Care/ Utilities	Average Cost (Euros)
1 month worth of electricity, gas, heaters etc.	215.35 €
1 month of Internet connection	29.10 €

Sports/ Leisure	Average Cost (Euros)
Fitness Club membership for 1 month	28. 25 €
International films - 1 seat	10.70 €

Childcare	Average Cost (Euros)
Pre – school (private) 1 child per month	297 €
International primary school 1 child per year	15, 600 €

Rent per Month	Average Cost (Euros)
1 Bedroom Apartment (in a city – center)	692 €
1 Bedroom Apartment (outside of city – center)	515 €

Rent per Month	Average Cost (Euros)
3 Bedroom Apartment (in a city – center)	1,350 €
3 Bedroom Apartment (outside of city – center)	984 €

Purchase of Apartment	Average Cost (Euros)
Price per square of apartments in city - center	4, 543 €
Price per square of apartments outside of city - center	3,057 €

Chapter Three: Expat Hubs and Cost of Living in Germany

Chapter Four: Renting vs. Buying a House

Finding a house to buy, or an apartment to rent always begins with finding a good location. Location is the first and foremost factor that any buyer or renter like you should consider and this is tied up to the purpose of your stay. Lots of expats come to the country to work, study, or do business which is why the apartment that they choose to rent or the house they choose to buy is usually near their working place, or school. Expats who come here for the sole purpose of pleasure (retired individuals, family reunification, young people looking to experience a different way of living etc.) usually move to top German cities especially for expats whose money is not an issue.

The length of your stay is the next factor to consider after location, housing options, and your financial capacity. The decision whether to rent or buy will differ; if you're only going to stay in the country because of your working contract, it'll be wise if you just rent since your contract may just last for a year or two.

If you're a student, and you have plans of going back to your home country after graduation, renting is also ideal. However, if you have a relationship with a German partner, or you and your spouse are looking to retire in the country then buying a house could be more ideal since you'd be staying for the long – term.

If you're only planning to stay for the short – term, say for only a few years, renting apartments are ideal. It's much easier to move in and out, and most of the apartments are located in city – centers and major public transportations making your move convenient plus you can easily adjust to your new environment.

The upside of getting an apartment is that you only move with you the most important things you'll need since you only have limited space. If you're going to relocate to the country, and you're going to bring your family with you, it'll be another factor you need to consider.

This chapter will guide you with regards to renting vs. buying a house in Germany.

Renting in Germany

It's essential to know German terminologies and norms once you set out to find a place to live in. For instance, if you wish to rent 2 bedrooms with a dining and living room, you're actually looking for a 4 – room home or *Vier Zimmer.* If you are looking for furnished apartments, it's very rare and will obviously cost more than an unfurnished one. Unfurnished apartments in Germany doesn't come with built – in closets and lighting fixtures, and sometimes even a kitchen sink which means that you're just renting or buying the house/ space itself, and you need to basically buy everything including appliances, lights, beds, tables, etc.

We highly recommend that you hire a legal advisor before you sign any lease because even if you can understand German, the contract are usually too long and the legal terms may be hard to comprehend in layman's term. On the other hand, it's your responsibility to take care of matters that aren't spelled out in the leasing contract. The essential parts of a landlord – tenant relationship are codified in a law. There could be nothing in the lease that states regarding notice periods, or actions required in the event of non – payment etc. but these matters are still covered because of the law.

Keep in mind that a contract to rent a house/ apartment for a fixed term cannot be terminated until the due date except under reasonably valid circumstances – relocating to a new state is not considered a valid circumstance.

Rental payments are usually made on a monthly basis. It also has 2 parts: the rent (this can't be changed for the duration of your lease; and the *Umlagen* - or *Nebenkosten* - which can. The latter usually includes payment for trash collection, share of landlord's property tax, water, heat, parking among others. If the costs of such items are raised during the period covered in your lease contract, the *Umlagen* can be increased accordingly. You will need to pay separately for house utilities like gas and electricity but sometimes it can be included in the *Umlagen*.

Common House Rules for Leasers

Here is some house rules that you need to keep in mind if you will reside in a rented quarter:

- Make sure that you have a document/ inventory/ receipt/ record/ of anything that should be noted in your place so that any possible deficiencies could be noted, and you have proof to show to your landlord.

- Renters should avoid loud sounds or too much noise especially around 1 to 3 PM, and 10 PM to 7 AM every day especially on Sundays (since this is like a rest day for everyone).

- Most cities in Germany require that the garbage should be separated properly. There are separate garbage cans (for metal/ plastic; paper; glass etc.) located in your landlord's property as well as in the sidewalk. If ever you need to throw something big like old furniture, you need to call the sanitation office to request for its removal. This is done on *Sperrmüll* or large trash day. Most states in Germany can also haul a car by appointment.

- You can wash and dry your clothes in laundry areas that are designated by your landlord. Cleaning blankets, carpets, rugs, and the likes should also be done in proper areas.

- Leave your bike/s, car/s, etc. in designated areas assigned by your landlord.

- If you have a pet or would want to keep one, you need to first ask your landlord if it's allowed, and acquire a written permission.

- The entrance doors are usually kept close from 9 PM to 7 AM if more than 1 family resides in the building.

- Make sure to lock your windows and doors if you're going to leave the apartment/ house for an extended period.

- If you need to install any TV antennas or satellite dishes, make sure to ask permission from your landlord, and also ask your district if it's allowed.

- You should inform your landlord as soon as possible if there are any damages to electrical lines, gas or water.

- Make sure to find out who is in charge of cleaning the stairway, hallway, lawn etc. because it could be you. Clarify it in your leasing contract.

- Do not create an open fire or grill on a balcony.

- Do not pour liquid or anything out your balcony, and if you're going to have flowerpots on your window or balcony, make sure that they are secure especially when you water your plants so that it wouldn't disturb your neighbors below.

Finding Rent

There are various approaches when it comes to finding a place to reside in the country. The easiest way is through a real estate agent (*Immobilienhändler*). Laws are constantly changing when it comes to paying real estate agents. Back then, the renter should pay for any substantial fees to the real estate agent, but now those fees are to be paid by the landlord. The effects are quite difficult to predict for property owners and real estate agents, so make sure to check who or how you're going to pay your agent before signing any contract.

Another way to search for a place to live in is through the internet or newspaper but be careful of the ads you see and make sure that it is legit and not a scam especially online. There are lots of legit real estate websites that would be useful for you. You can easily check out the available listings, the price, size, location etc. Photographs of the house/ apartment are also uploaded to entice prospective renters.

The third method is simply through word of mouth. Sometimes it's the best way to find a good and affordable place. You may want to network out to some locals, or you can ask your colleagues/ friends who are already residing in Germany for any recommendations.

When it comes to making a deposit, it's usually 2 to 3 months' rent in addition to your first month's rent. Your initial deposit or down - payment will be returned when you leave, usually with interest, provided that the apartment or house you live in is in good order.

Apartment/House Rental Terms

Finding apartment in the country is easier than ever, thanks to the internet. However, the terms used to describe the apartment or house you're looking to rent may confuse you even if you can already understand German. This is very true with abbreviations that are used in newspaper ads which is why this section will give you some keywords for you to better understand the terms:

- **QM** or **M2** (Quadratmeter): this abbreviation comes with a number indicating how big the house is in square meters. Zimmer (Zi) comes with a number that indicates how many rooms the apartment has.

- **BJ** (Baujahr): This term followed by a number indicates what year is the apartment building was built.

- **WC** (Water Closet), **Du** (Dusche), **Bad** (Bathroom): Indicates the sanitary facilities included. Bath only means a tub, and the water closet refers to a toilet only with no bathtub.

- **EG** (Erdgeschoss): Ground floor
- **OG** (Obergeschoss): Upper floor
- **DG** (Dachgeschos): Attic floor

- **Ka**, **Kt** and **Kaut** (Kaution): Security Deposit; it's followed by a number which indicates how much you need to pay in euros.

- **NK** (Nebenkosten): This refers to incidental expenditures that aren't included in your lease (ex: parking, garage, balcony, trash, water, stairwell/ hallway cleaning, garden etc.)

Buying a House in Germany

Unlike most countries, Germans prefer to buy houses and keep it for good. They do not buy a house and continuously upgrade later as with most non – European practices, this is why there are real estate market doesn't fluctuate as much, though the demand for location is high.

It's typical for would – be homeowners to take their time when finding a house to buy. With this in mind, it's best if you invest or buy a home in areas that are located in a place where there is good infrastructure because even if you buy it at a high price, the property will appreciate over the long term and will be worth more.

Only 46% of Germans own their houses; the country has the lowest percentage of homeowners in the whole European Union. Expats could increase the rate of homeownership in the future since there are no legal restrictions on non – Germans owning a house or property, and usually foreign nationals have high income and they also have goals of buying their own house. Perhaps the only hindrance for an expat to own a property is the financial institutions. Since there's no financial track record yet, the mortgages that these banks will offer are higher than average.

Housing Costs

Before we delve deeper into this topic, it's important to note that the size of houses in Germany, and most countries in the European Union, is relatively smaller compared to those that are built in North America. Germany only has about 1/9th living space compared to the 1/35th in the

U.S., much of this living space is also developed which is why cost of residence tends to be much higher.

It's also important to note that the houses or apartments in the country are usually built very well, and quality materials were used since the builders need to adhere to strict building laws.

The prices of houses and apartments vary greatly throughout the country, especially within each federal state. Just like in any other countries, prices of housing in the countryside or those already far away from metropolitan/ touristy areas tend to be much lower.

Many of the real estate websites you'll find online provides prospective buyers with a breakdown of regional/ city prices for both homes and apartments. The prices are listed on a real estate company's websites, and most of them update their database so that buyers can track or see the prices of their house listings over time, and get updated on any significant market movements.

The average price of a typical single – detached home with a size of about 140 to 180 sq. meters inclusive of garage is mostly below €260,000 though expect that the price vary from one region to another.

In the western regions of the country, here is the average price of some states/ cities:

- Rheinland - Pfalz: €209,000
- Nordrhein-Westfalen: €253,700
- Saarland: €196,000

In the eastern regions of the country, here is the average price of some states/ cities:

- Sachsen: €241,500
- Brandenburg: €253,500
- Sachsen-Anhalt: €177.800

In the southern regions of the country, here is the average price of some states/ cities:

- Bayern: €333,000
- Baden-Württemberg: €313,000

For the state of Hessen which is located in Germany's central region, the average price of a single – detached house is €258,000. The houses in the city – state of Bremen are one of the cheapest among the major cities in Germany; a 150 sq. meter is around €265,000. Other major cities like Bavaria (capital of Munich) is by far the most expensive; 100 sq. meters of living space can cost a whopping €900,000 while a much smaller house may cost €500,000 which is still very expensive especially for average income earners.

Here are the average prices of a 150 sq. meter housing in other major cities:

- Frankfurt: €525,000
- Hamburg: €467,000

- Berlin: €337,650

- Düsseldorf: €491,000

Buying an Apartment

If you're going to buy an apartment instead of a single – detached house, the average price per sq. meter will cost around €2,230. The same price variables for housing properties for each city or state tend to be the same with apartments. Smaller apartments tend to cost relatively more per square meter of living space.

How to Find and Buy a House or Apartment

Just like in other countries in Europe, there are certain steps you need to take for you to find the right house or apartment and close a sale. In Germany, the property owners do not have a "For Sale" signage in front of the house because Germans offer their properties through publishing it in newspapers, online, or through a real estate agent. There are lots of websites that you can go to in order to get a review of house and apartment listings for sale including rental units. Some websites also provides prospective buyers with information regarding financing, mortgage, contracts or any matter related to renting or buying a property.

There are some home or property owners that are private sellers (von privat) which mean that no real estate agent is involved but most homeowners offer their property with the help of real estate agents (Immobilienmakler). You must thoroughly research the property if you're considering of buying it because sometimes the advertisements are misleading the buyer; inexpensive houses usually require renovation investments that could go beyond the purchase cost.

Another warning sign in the ads is grosszügige Räume which pertains to "very spacious or large rooms," this could mean that it will be more expensive to heat. You should also watch out for properties listed that are for quick decision-makers (*für Schnellentschlossene)* because this could mean that the property is not desirable or it could have been on the market for a very long time.

House – hunting is usually a hassle for prospective buyers especially if you find one from newspaper or print ads because some of them do not give addresses and you need to set up an appointment to check out the house. Thanks to the internet, many websites now lists not just addresses but also maps of the house/ apartment.

We highly recommend that you shouldn't sign any exclusivity contract with any real estate agent because you wouldn't want to be deprived of the various offers coming from several agents. On the onset, ask your agent regarding the percentage of his/ her commission. There's no law regulating commissions except for rental contracts but this could change; in most instances, the commission is around 3 to 7% of the purchase price. Sometimes, the buyer pays the full amount of commission while most split it between the buyer and seller though there are real estate agents receiving their full commission directly from the seller.

An agent may only submit an invoice once he/ she have already confirmed the transaction between both parties. This means that the agent already gave the buyer the full address, and contact details of the seller as well as the purchase price.

It's also wise to ask the seller whether he/ she already have a contract with any other agent. You can also ask the seller on how much commission should be given since the seller has a fair idea of what the agent had done to sell his/her house. The buyer can also ask the agent what he/ she have done to earn the fee that he/she is charging.

Keep in mind that if a prospective buyer gets an offer from one agent that another has already offered, it's best to tell the second agent as soon as possible otherwise the buyer might end up paying a double commission.

Once a property has been found, expect that there'll be additional expenses which are estimated at around 10% of the purchase price. In addition to the commission for the real estate agent, you should also include within your budget the notary fee, property transfer tax, administrative expenses, hiring an interpreter (for the contract signing verbatim) etc.

The property transfer tax may cost around 4 to 6% of the purchase price. The higher the purchase price, the higher tax price there will be. After the taxes, you need to also pay a notary fee; once the buyer and seller have agreed on a purchase price, a notary or lawyer should be present during the signing of property sales contract. This is beneficial especially for the buyer because it provides assurance that the transaction is done in accordance with the law. Notary fees may cost around 1.5 to 2%, and the lawyer usually covers the preparation of the contract, land register, transfer of name, signing ceremony, and other negotiations.

Notary Duties and Responsibilities

The notary functions as an impartial middleman between the buyer and seller of the property. It is his or her duty to check if the land or property that's registered can be sold or not; and if there would be any restrictions on its use.

The contract will state all the obligations of each party as well as the measures that need to be taken in the event of a default. Once the contract is signed, the notary shall register the change of ownership at the local government, and he/she must enter the property in the land register. Many expats choose their own notary, so you might want to get someone who speaks English, or one that resonates with you.

Make sure to ask for a copy of the purchase contract for the house before you go to your legal advisor, review it thoroughly and have it translated for you if need be. Prepare any questions you may have, and don't hesitate to ask your notary about it so that you can fully understand the conditions you're agreeing with.

At the actual signing of the contract, the notary/ lawyer will read the contract of sale verbatim for the buyer and seller to make sure that everything is clear for both parties. You as the buyer can ask any question that arises and discuss it during the signing ceremony if a certain clause isn't clear. It's important to note that the reading is done in

German, so if you are not yet fully proficient with the language, make sure that you hire a professional interpreter, though there will be additional costs.

In most cases, both parties are not individuals but spouses, or even family owners; it is best that everyone involved is present at the contract signing. You should also bring your passports for identification.

The Contract

These are the essential things that you should take note in the contract:

- Names and addresses of both the buyer and seller are correctly noted as well as the details of the property being bought. Make sure to thoroughly check it because sometimes there are errors in the property details which could make the contract partially invalidated.

- The agreed upon terms and conditions of payment as well as the purchase price.

- Stipulations as to what happens in the event that either party fails to comply to the terms and conditions of the contract.

- The buyer and seller usually have complete freedom to decide on payment terms and conditions. Usually, the buyer has to obtain financing for the property or house; therefore the seller should agree to a priority notice in the land register. This will protect the buyer from other sale activities like when a seller tries to sell the property to other buyers for a better price.

- The land register is where the document (containing all essential information for ownership) for a property can be retrieved; it is located in the district courthouse. An actual change in ownership can only happen once the entry has been changed in the land register, and only when the tax has already certified that the seller has no outstanding property taxes, and if the previous mortgages are already accomplished.

In most cases, the purchase price is paid into the account that's maintained by the notary. The money is only transferred to the seller once the land register is already completed.

It's important to note that the notary isn't responsible for the correctness of the property description which means that it is the buyer's responsibility to make sure that the description is correct. The seller is also not obliged to point out any major defects in the property that should have been obvious to the buyer, though the seller should be required to list any hidden defects.

A copy of the latest land register can be retrieved from the district court, but the only people eligible to make the application are the ones who are legitimately involved like the owner of the property or the notary public. The register should also state the rights of any third parties (if any). For instance, if there are tenants in the property; the tenants can't bar the sale of the property but the new homeowner is still bound by any contracts to which the previous owner agreed to. This could mean that the new owner can't evict a tenant until the expiration date of the lease.

Financing Your House or Apartment

It's very likely that the prospective buyer can't pay in full right away which is why the buyer needs time to finance. Of course, if you're the buyer, you shouldn't buy a property that is way beyond your budget or financial resources. 20% of the total cost is the usual recommendation for making a down – payment.

Recent regulations for the banking industry require bankers to take a closer look at property ownership in Germany particularly those whose earnings are in some other currency. As a result, there could be stricter rules for mortgages.

Mortgages

Interest rates for mortgages range between 1.15% and 2.30%, depending on certain conditions. Most mortgages are usually paid for 10 to 20 years. Take note that these are all subject to change.

There is stability in interest rates with only slight fluctuations, so it's possible to lessen the total amount of interest through paying it up front. The greater the payment, the less interest it will incur in the long term. Sometimes, the seller may transfer his mortgage to the buyer which could be an advantage for the buyer since the mortgage rates acquired may have been lower.

When it comes to financing, it's very wise to seek specialized advice, or hire a tax consultant/ bank specialist. The purchase of a house or construction can be subsidized by the government but under certain conditions. You could also get some tax advantages. The people who are more likely to benefit from such subsidies are those with average income and with minor children; this is where a professional advice from a bank/ tax consultant comes in handy.

There are further regulations when it comes to financing and acquiring mortgages from German banks so make sure to inquire and check what needs to be done because the regulations of bank/ financial institutions greatly vary, and seek help from professionals.

Chapter Five: Utilities and Communication Services in Germany

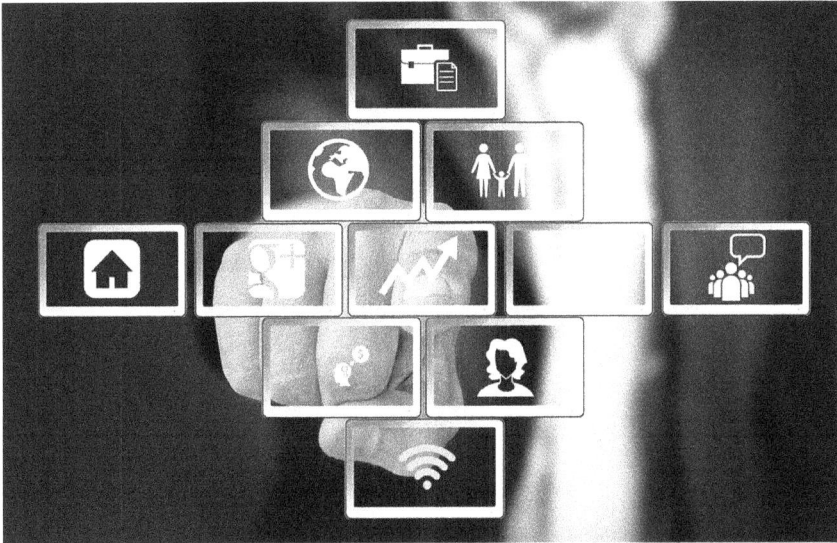

This chapter will give you a primer on the basics of relocating into your new home. Once all the paperwork for the lease or the house you bought is done, your things have been shipped, and you're finally ready to move, the next step to take care of the utilities in your new household such as telecommunication services, water, electricity, and heating/ gas. Your utility responsibilities will depend on your lease agreement.

If you bought a house, the kind of services that you need could already be set – up or installed, and what you need to do is to just transfer the billing details from the previous owner to you.

Contracts and Payments

This section will cover the basic utility services, and how it can be set – up; finding new providers, setting up/ transferring contracts, billing or payment methods, and installation.

Gas/ Heating

If you are renting a house or an apartment, the landlord determines how much you should pay depending on the heat source installed and the size of the apartment. Sometimes, the apartments/ houses has radiators for temperature heating as well as other heat sources for cooking such as liquid gas, natural gas etc. Expect that the costs will vary every year based on your consumption as well as price increases. Your landlord is the one responsible for choosing a gas supplier; most likely the owner of the building is connected with a certain gas supplier. You can still choose to have your own gas supplier but make sure to discuss it during negotiations with your landlord, and perhaps you need to include it in the leasing contract.

Electricity

Each rental houses and apartments have an electricity meter; this means that you, as the tenant, is the one responsible to set up an account with the electric provider so that it will be directly billed to you. The meter should already be installed and ready once the tenant moves in. Electricity bills are usually paid every month or every 2 months. It must be paid through a standing order from the bank, though there could also be other payment options. Initially, the amount to be paid is fixed, and it's only adjusted after 1 year based on your consumption. Meters are usually read once a year. Regardless if you choose a different electric provider or not, you must strictly settle your bills on the due date. You should also discuss with your landlord if you would like to have a different supplier, and make sure to include in your leasing contract.

When it comes to houses, it's pretty much the same with renting in apartment building. You need to sign up for an account with your chosen electric provider, and the billing is directly addressed to you. In some cases, you may need to just transfer the billing contract of the previous owner under your name. There are various electric companies to choose from since the electricity market in the country had been de – regulated. If you choose to change your electric supplier, keep in mind that there could be a notice period required, and this could vary from one company to another.

Water Supply

Water is supplied by the municipal waterworks, and it's usually included in the rental. Your landlord determines the cost based on your water consumption. Just like electricity, water meters are read once a year, and the cost is adjusted for the next 12 months. Most rental units have their own water meters. If ever that the place you are renting don't have one, the water bill could be based on the size of your apartment (depending on the sq. meters). How water consumption is billed and/ or paid is stated in your leasing contract.

If you're going to rent or buy a house, the water metering system are already installed. If not, you may need to sign up for an account with the local waterworks. This would require a water meter reading once you've moved in, and you need to also talk with the local authorities to have your account set – up. Billing is usually done every 2 months, and paid via bank. The payment every 2 months is adjusted after 1 year based on your consumption through a meter reading once a year.

Telephone/ Internet Connections

The tenant is the one responsible for setting up the telephone and internet connections. There are lots of telecom providers that offer a wide range of plans to suit every customer's needs. We recommend that you check first the plan of the service provider you like so that you can learn what type of internet service is best for you. Some cities have high – speed DSL lines while other cities already have fiber optic lines. It's also possible to get your telecom/ internet connection from your cable TV provider and register for a package plan. If you want less hassle, you can just take over the existing connection of the previous tenant or owner. However, make sure to check the details of the contract of the existing connection, and inform your landlord or the previous owner so that you will have no problems.

Payments are usually made through a Direct Debit via your bank. A Direct Debit is different from a Standing Order because the amounts taken out vary every month.

Do take note that the speed and services of your provider may vary from one area to another. In rural places, there could be no high – speed internet available because high – speed lines may not be installed which is why some people get internet via setting up a dish satellite.

Expect a 2 – week delay until the internet/ phone line is up. Most internet/ telecom providers in Germany will want you to sign a 2 year contract so if you're only going to stay in the country temporarily, make sure to just sign up for a monthly contract that you can cancel anytime for a charge.

Here are some of the internet providers in Germany and their basic internet/ mobile plans. Do take note that the plans and rates are subject to change:

Internet Providers and Basic Plans

1&1

They are the most widely known internet service provider in the country. 1 &1 also offers reasonable internet plans and a steady network performance of around 50 Megabits per second. The company's internet connection comes with a quality router as well.

Basic Plan Rate: Internet connection @ 16 Megabits per second for €14.99

O2

O2 offers one of the cheapest options for internet services in Germany. The only complaint that most expats have with this company is their customer service but overall, you can get a great package deal for an affordable price. Keep in mind though that their lowest internet plans come with long – term contracts.

Basic Plan Rate: Internet connection + phone line @ 16 Megabits per second for €19.99

Telekom (Deutsche Telekom/ T- Home)

Telekom is a widely known internet and telecom service provider in the country. They deliver the best internet/ phone services and they are also reputable for having an excellent customer service though their plans are relatively expensive.

Basic Plan Rate: Internet connection @ 16 Megabits per second for €29.95

Vodafone

Vodafone is a company from the U.K that offers telecom services in Germany. You can get bundled options (internet, cable, mobile/ phone lines) for a relatively cheap price of €27.90. However, the company's network is not as extensive compared to other service providers in Germany.

Basic Plan Rate: Internet connection + Cable + phone/ mobile plans for €27.90.

Vodafone also offer bundled mobile plans @ €29.95

Mobile Basic Plan Options

Provider: Vodafone

- Plan: Red XL
- Plan Type: Postpaid
- Data in Gigabyte: Unlimited
- Price per month: €79.99
- Extras: Unlimited Calls and Texts

Provider: O2

- Plan: O2 Free Unlimited
- Plan Type: Postpaid
- Data in Gigabyte: Unlimited
- Price per month: € 59.99
- Extras: Unlimited Calls and Texts

Provider: Sim Discount

- Plan: All Net Flat 10GB LTE
- Plan Type: Postpaid
- Data in Gigabyte: 10
- Price per month: €19.99
- Extras: Unlimited Calls and Texts

Provider: Blau

- Plan: AllNet XL
- Plan Type: Postpaid (24 months)
- Data in Gigabyte: 5
- Price per month: € 14.99
- Extras: Unlimited Calls and Texts

Provider: Aldi Talk

- Plan: Paket M

- Plan Type: Prepaid

- Data in Gigabyte: 3

- Price per month: € 12.99

- Extras: Unlimited Calls and Texts

Provider: Telekom

- Plan: Magenta Mobil Start M

- Plan Type: Prepaid

- Data in Gigabyte: 1

- Price per month: € 9.95

- Extras: Free Data Roaming in Switzerland and other

  European countries

Provider: McSIM

- Plan: LTE Mini SMS 1 GB

- Plan Type: Postpaid

- Data in Gigabyte: 1

- Price per month: € 5.99

- Extras: 100 min.

Relocation Services

If you think that finding out a place to rent, relocating, utilities, address change, contracts etc. are overwhelming; you can hire specialists to take care of such things for you. There are companies who offer a wide range of services related to relocation.

Individuals as well as small and large businesses moving abroad often seek out help from these specialists. Usually, they can take care of tasks such as house hunting, address registration, working permits, residence permits, utilities arrangement, phone services, and banking connections. In addition to these services, some also offer cultural and language training, career counseling, driver's license, health insurance, medical connections, and pretty much all the necessary thing that any person/ company will need once they make the move.

The relocation industry is becoming more and more in demand and many of the companies that offer such services have already formed partnerships with various firms within Germany, and the rest of Europe. There are also international relocation companies around the world to meet the demands of expats.

You might want to consider getting help so that the transition will be less stressful for you/ your family. Search online and sign on with a company that will suit your needs and budget. It will surely be worth it and relocation will not be a hassle.

Chapter Six: Work and Business in Germany

The export industry particularly the logistics sector as well as the automobile/ manufacturing industries offer lots of vacancies for both locals and expats who wanted to get a stable job in the country. Germany is also continuously offering various positions in the medical field particularly doctors and healthcare personnel. Many expats also work in the hotel management field and gastronomy industries. This doesn't mean that other sectors or fields of work aren't hiring because there are thousands of positions in administrative fields, science and technology, academics, trades, and the likes.

Finding a Job in Germany

If your residence permit allows you to work in the country, there are various ways on where you can find jobs easily and legitimately – thanks to the internet.

For specialists/ skilled laborers, and executive level positions one of the best way to begin your search is through an executive search firm (Personalberatung). The service is free for candidates who are searching for such positions plus the main advantage of turning to an executive search firm is that you don't have to be in Germany to start your job hunting.

If you want to see extensive listing of job vacancies, you can check out Bundesagentur für Arbeit; this service is also free, and you can also check the status of your job application online. They also have International Placement Services branches throughout the country to help expats. You can check out their website at <www.arbeitsagentur.de>

Another option for job hunters is to apply for work through temporary employment agencies. The role of these agencies is to supply workers to various companies in Germany that they are associated with. Make sure to thoroughly read all the legalities involved particularly in your residence permit, taxes, employment contracts, and benefits if you are planning to get work through an employment agency.

Hiring Procedures and Employment Contract

Working in Germany for an expat like you means that you need to become familiar with the hiring process. You also need to learn what should be included in your employment contract once you've been offered one so that you can know what to expect.

Step #1: Application and Curriculum Vitae

A written job application consists of curriculum vitae (CV)/ resume and cover letter. You also need to attach copies of the needed documents or certificates to prove to your employer that you are qualified for the job, and you can legally work in the country. References should also be provided even if your previous job is in another country.

Make sure that you attached a photo (usually 2x2 or depending on what photo size your employer will require) on your application as well.

Your application should be clearly organized since this is how you're going to make a good first impression. The copies documents or certificates attach should be clear and of high quality; don't forget to also bring the original copies for verification.

Thanks to the internet, applications can be submitted online with ease. In fact, most companies prefer job hunters to submit their applications online. There are two ways on how you can submit your application online – via email attachment, or through filling out a form via the company's website. You can also check out some websites that offer services where you can see the status of your job application though this may not be applicable to all companies.

With regards to the Curriculum Vitae, the content must be structured, and it should contain the applicant's professional profile and personal information. One of the things that applicants fail to do in their CV is finding the right balance of professional information. Here are some tips:

- Avoid listing every single job you've ever had. Keep in mind that the hiring manager will only want to see what could be relevant / related to the position you're applying for. Irrelevant career stages should best be left out, and only list the jobs or positions that could be of any interest for your potential employer.

- Make sure to accurately describe what your tasks are in the positions you have listed. It's best to list 3 to 5 major responsibilities from your previous job/s that could help your application.

- Attach a portrait photo on your CV. Most expats don't know that adding a professional portrait photo to a CV increases their chances of getting an interview. Attaching a photo is the norm for applicants in the country.

Step #2: Interview

Once your application made an impression to the hiring manager or potential employer, they will obviously invite you over for a job interview to get to know you better. If you lie to your potential employer, you will definitely lose your job and your contract will be terminated on the grounds of fraudulent deception.

Here are some questions that the interviewer/ employer are NOT allowed to ask a candidate since such questions/ topics could be seen as a violation of the General Equal Treatment Act. It is however allowed if it constitutes a job requirement:

- Female applicants are not allowed to be asked whether she is pregnant or not.
- Race
- Gender/ Sexual Identity
- Ethnic Origin
- Disability
- Religion
- Criminal Record (though this is allowed if it's relevant to the position/ employment relationship).

Interview expenses like travel, accommodation, meals etc. are usually covered by the employer though it depends on the company. Some employer could indicate that they will not provide the reimbursement of all the costs entailed in the invitation letter but this should be clearly stated in the letter that they will send you.

The Employment Contract

Negotiations are freely done between the employers and employees. The negotiations can be concluded orally (only for small matters) but in most cases, it is put down in writing. Once you get hired, your employer should provide you a copy of a written employment contract to ensure that you are officially an employee of the company. The employment contract should include the following terms:

- Job Description
- Start and duration of employment
- Trial or Probation Period
- Remuneration/ Compensation package
- Working hours
- Days of holidays

- Period of Notice

- Company agreements (if applicable)

- Benefits included

- Other important terms

Remunerations are perhaps the most important terms in an employment contract. You need to check the contract if your employer will pay bonuses in addition to your salary, or if they will pay over – time payments etc. The contract should clearly state when you will be paid (ex: every 1st of the month, end of the month, twice a month, daily etc.). It must also state the employee's gross salary so that one can see how much will be deducted for social contributions, health insurance, pension/ retirement, unemployment insurance, tax etc.

If applicable, the contract must clearly state if the position is for a fixed term only. Should an employer fail to do so, then the employment agreement is deemed to have been concluded for an unlimited time. In most cases, the contract of employment is valid for an unlimited period but it's also possible that some positions are concluded for a limited period only (fixed term contract) – the duration for such contract is in accordance with the completion of a certain task, occurrence of a specific circumstance, or specific end date.

The fixed term contract should also be based on a justification that the position or work is only for a temporary requirement, or as a replacement of an absent employee.

If an employee wants to claim the ineffectiveness of a limited contract, one should take legal action within 3 weeks after the end of the contract.

During the first 4 years after the start – up of a company, employment contracts can be concluded on a fixed – term basis without reasonable justifications for a 4 year period.

Self – Employment in Germany

Self – employment in Germany depends on the kind of residence permit that you have. It's impossible and illegal for a foreign national to engage in any business activities wherein they are self – employed.

We highly recommend that you inquire first with a legal adviser if the permit you have allows you to become self – employed. You can also ask those who are experts in labor, taxation, and business before you even attempt on doing any self – employed work.

Residence permits that allows expats to work in the country is usually easily acquired by professionals who are either a specialist in their field, or those with sought – after labor expertise such as professional experts, researchers/ scientists, specific executive level positions etc. though other qualified professionals can also acquire work and residence permits.

If you are serious about relocating in the country, and would want to become a self – employed expat, you must meet the requirements of a residence permit that will allow you to do so. You and even your family can acquire this type of working permit provided that you can show the German authorities that your business or self – employed profession will benefit the locals, and in a broader picture, the German economy.

The criteria involved in getting a residence permit that will allow you to conduct to become self – employed usually depends on the type of your business, your professional qualifications, and whether or not you could be doing something that can be done by a local or other qualified professionals.

The Foreigners Office in Germany will most likely ask you to submit various paperworks, and check with the local Chamber of Commerce if your business is economically viable and/ or specialized enough to become sustainable. If the local authorities deemed your business as acceptable, then you won't have any problem acquiring a residence permit.

Keep in mind though that even if you are allowed for self – employment, there could be some limitations as to where you can conduct your business, and what you can do. Needless to say, your working permit may restrict you from doing business in a certain geographical area; this decision will depend on the German authorities. It is highly recommended that you ask help from a legal advisor to see whether certain business/ self – employment restrictions can be changed or not.

If you're relocating in the country as a self – employed individual, and you're going to bring your spouse or family with you, then you/ your family will most likely need to take additional steps so that you can be permitted to set up your own business.

Another thing that you should be aware of before you can work in Germany as a self – employed individual is that your professional qualifications must be recognized by the German government. You can inquire at the German Federal Government regarding this matter.

Once you've completed and sorted out your residence permit inquiries, the next step is to register and establish your business. The exact classification of your work should be determined because rules and regulations may vary depending on the type of business you are engaged in. Just like acquiring residence permits, this process can be a bit tedious. Make sure to ask for professional help or legal assistance to clarify where your profession or business fits in.

Free – Professionals/ Freelancers

Free – Professionals or self – employed individuals are those who have academic training such as physicians, lawyers, pharmacists, dentists etc. Other free – professions can be considered as "trades" while others are under the "crafts" including barbers, butchers, florists and the likes. There are also the so – called "freelancers" who are becoming more and more popular because of online jobs; it includes writers, virtual assistants, graphic artists as well as those who are independent consultants, performers, and artists.

Your work classification is very important because it will determine what type of tax you pay and how much. It will also affect the licenses or certificates you need to have as well as whether or not you need to be a member of a professional groups or become associated with other "chambers."

For instance, you want to be engage in a work that's classified as a "trade," then make sure to check the requirements at your local Trades Office because you may need to acquire a certificate of registration to officially register your business. To get such certificate, you need to show that you're a qualified individual with a credible and reliable character to operate your business. Having a certificate of registration also entails an self – employed individual to pay the local trade tax, and requires you to become a member of the local Chamber of Commerce. As a member, you are obligated to pay a membership fee annually.

Free - professionals could be exempted from certain registration procedures though there would be certain regulations that one needs to follow.

To engage in "Crafts" means that a self – employed individual needs the approval of a trade association because this will establish and verify that one met the German standards related to one's chosen craft or qualifications.

Freelancers are under a different category and have a somewhat different set of rules and regulations as well as registration procedures to follow.

Important Note:

Seeking help from an expert or a legal advisor regarding self – employment in the country can't be stressed enough because the rules, procedures, and regulations are always subject to change. It will be a great advantage that you have someone who knows the rules so that you won't get into misunderstandings and trouble in the long run.

Doing Business in Germany

Being one of the largest economic powerhouses in the world, Germany is a place where business and start – ups thrives. The country is home to thousands of businesses ranging from sole proprietors to huge local and international companies. Part of the reason why the country's economy is prominent in the world is because of the SMEs or Small – Medium Sized businesses. This is because the government is very open to all types of establishments regardless if the owner is a local or a foreigner. In this section, we will discuss the different categories of companies in Germany so that you can properly register your business.

Types of Business Structures

Individuals or businesses that have intentions of engaging in commercial activities in the country may choose to establish a corporate entity. Some companies that haven't yet established any presence in Germany usually assign an agent to operate the business on their behalf through establishing a corporation. Advice from legal advisors as well as business experts is very important before deciding what kind of structure is best suited for one's business. Check out the business structure in Germany below:

Sole Proprietorship

This is the most common type of business structure especially for many expats. Sole proprietorship comes next after a corporation – type of businesses. It's the most suitable structure for self – employed people, entrepreneurs as well as freelance professionals. Sole proprietorship refers to businesses run by only a single individual who must have the right residence/ working permit. There's unlimited liability – this means that the owner will bear all the responsibilities concerning the business/ company, or he/she is solely liable.

Limited Liability Company (GmBH - Gesellschaft mit beschränkter Haftung)

This is the most common type of company structure in the country. Under this category, the shareholders are not liable for any of the company's debts. Shareholders can set up a Limited Liability Company provided that the share capital is at least €25,000. A notarized agreement is written between the legal existence of the company, and the shareholder. The company's legal identity only begins once it is officially registered in the Commercial Register.

The name of the company/ business must be from the name of the shareholders or the business purpose of the enterprise. It should also contain the addendum LLC or mit beschränkter Haftung.

Do take note that shares of the GmBH or LLC cannot be quoted in a stock exchange, and it cannot be embodied in a certificate as well though the shares can be transferred to someone by adhering to certain regulations and submitting notarized documents. There should be one or more

managing directors appointed in a GmBh, and it must be

only those individuals who are either entitled to legally

represent the company, or one of the shareholders.

Joint – Stock Company (AG – Aktiengesellschaft)

The company should at least have 5 members to set

up this kind of company structure. The share capital that's

required should be at least €50,000. The shares could be but

need not be listed on the stock exchange. For a business to

set up an AG, they should submit articles of association

that's authenticated by a notary public or through a court.

The company only becomes a separate legal entity once it

has been officially registered in the Commercial Register.

Just like GmBH, the name of the company/ business must be

from the name of the shareholders, or the business purpose

of the enterprise. It should also contain the addendum AG or

Aktiengesellschaft.

A joint – stock company should have an appointed

managing board that have the responsibility to decide on all

matters related to the operation of the company. The

managing board is also answerable to the supervisory board. The shareholders of a joint – stock company exercise their power through approving policies during shareholder's meetings or general meetings.

General Partnerships (OHG - Offene Handelsgesellschaft)

Compared to an LLC (GmBH) and a joint – stock company (AG), the partners in an OHG have unlimited liability. Each of the company's partner is legally obliged to actively participate in the business' operations unless the partner agreement provides otherwise. The General Partnerships structure is a company that can sue or be sued in a court of law. According to the Commercial Code, the decisions for internal matters should be unanimously made but some partnership agreements allow decisions to be made through majority of votes.

Limited Partnerships (KG – Kommanditgesellschaft)

This kind of structure provides a limitation of liability by having 2 kinds of partners:

- The General Partner: Has unlimited liability that is extended to his/ her personal assets.

- Limited Partner: Has a liability that only extends to his/ her nominal holdings in the company.

Limited Partnerships with a Limited Liability Company as a General Partner (GmBH & Co KG)

Based on the name of the structure, this is a combination of a Limited Liability Company with a Limited Partnership through making the LLC the general partner of the Limited Partnership. The limited partners are liable only to the extent of their registered nominal holdings.

Subsidiary (Töchtergesellschaft)

A subsidiary is an affiliation to another company or a foreign entity. It is still considered as a legally independent company which means that it has its own accounting system, business assets, management, and balance sheet processes.

Branch (Zweigniederlassung)

A branch is a legally dependent business/ company but is a financial independent wing of a head office that operates outside Germany.

Chapter Seven: Education System in Germany

The education system in Germany is quite different from the system of other countries, but the country has produced high – performing students. The majority of students in the country attend public schools including those who are foreign nationals. The education system including those in higher education is available to foreign nationals as well as the children of bona fide expats. Expect that the classes are conducted in German which is fine if one is just beginning school but could become a problem for expat students who are already in high school or college that aren't yet proficient in the language; this is why some expats choose to enroll themselves or their older children in private schools because the some classes are conducted in both German and English. Although education is a function of the federal states, the systems vary from one state to another but there could be some generalizations.

Children who are 3 to 6 years of age can attend pre – school or kindergarten. After this stage, school is compulsory for the next 9 to 10 years. From first to fourth grade children attend Grundschule (elementary school) where general subjects are taught. Once the student completed the 4th grade, they are already separated according to their academic ability, or depending on their parents/ family they can choose to attend any of the 3 types of schools:

- Hauptschule
- Realschule
- Gymnasium

The teachers usually give advice to students on what kind of school system they should attend based on their previous performance in school such as academic achievement, special abilities, self – confidence, other distinctive traits. In most states, the child's parents/ family is ultimately the one who decide as to which type of school their child should attend after the fourth grade.

Hauptschule (Grade 5 to Grade 9)

This type of school teaches pretty much the same subjects that are being taught in Realschule and Gymnasium, but in a much slower pace. Vocational – oriented courses are also being taught. This leads to a part – time admission in a vocational type of school with a combination of internship training until the student is 18 years old.

Realschule (Grade 5 to Grade 10)

In most cases, attending a realschule leads to part – time vocational courses, and also higher vocational school. Upon graduation, the students who achieved flying colors or have achieved high academic grades can switch to a Gymnasium school.

Gymnasium

Attending a Gymnasium school leads to acquiring a Abitur or a diploma. This type of school prepares the students for higher education/ university study, and also provides vocational and academic credentials. The curricula of Gymnasium school vary from one institution to another, though these are the subjects that are generally being taught:

- German language
- Physics
- Math
- Geography
- Arts (crafts/ design)
- History

- Chemistry

- Computer Science

- Biology

- Philosophy

- Music

- Social Studies

- Civics

- Foreign Languages

In the past years, some states in the country have changed the curriculum so that students can get an Abi or certification after completing the 12th grade. Other states are also making the transition but some still require a student to complete Grade 13.

Gesamtschule (Comprehensive School)

This type of educational system only exists in some states, and it comprises of grades 5 to 10. Comprehensive schools are somewhat a combination of a Hauptschule and Realschule. Students who excellently completed the comprehensive school until the 9th grade will receive a Hauptschule certificate while students who completed schooling until the 10th grade will receive a Realschule certificate.

Berufsschule

Berufsschule is a combination of part – time academic study and internship. Once the student successfully completed the internship program, he/ she will receive a certification in that particular field of work or trade. This type of school is different from the standard schooling system in Germany because it is controlled by the federal government, trade unions, and industry.

No matter what kind of school you or your kids attend, a student should complete at least 9 years of education. For instance, if a student drops out of a Gymnasium school system, he/ she must enrol in either a Realschule or Hauptschule until 9 years of basic education is completed. Students are also required to study at least 1 foreign language for 5 years. Gymnasium schools require studying a second foreign language as well.

For expats who have already completed the equivalent years of basic education in other countries, it depends on your school whether or not the education you've completed in your home country is credited.

The School Day

Classes in Germany usually start in the morning around 7:30 AM or 8:15 AM, and this can end between 12 noon and 1:30 in the afternoon. Class periods usually last for 45 minutes with a short break in between. There are some schools that offered longer school time and the students use the additional hours to do their homework, or joining extracurricular activities. The homework of the students is usually focused on reading, writing, and arithmetic. The curriculum of the student expands the level gets higher, but it depends on which of the 3 types of secondary schools will the student attend.

The School Year

There are 2 semesters in a school year; school begins around the 2nd week or 4th week of August. There are longer breaks during the holidays (around 2 weeks), and summertime (around 6 weeks), on the other hand, there are just shorter breaks during Easter and autumn. The exact dates of the school breaks are set by the individual schools. There's no school during public holidays;

Schools for Students who have Special Needs

For students who have special needs, there are different schools that one can attend to, and these are called Sonderschule or Förderschule. A student can attend one of these schools depending on the availability, and the individual's needs. These types of schools have teachers who are trained in special education. It generally has a small student to teacher ratio compared to regular schools.

Private Schools

There are lots of different types of private schools in the country. Private schools charge a school tuition fee, and some offers varied courses that could lead to a German diploma including other certifications upon graduation.

Internat (Boarding Schools)

Internat schools are boarding schools in the country. Lots of these institutions offer various study programs and/or specialized courses in various fields. They award diploma upon conclusion of studies, and also give students additional specialized certificates upon completion of specialized courses. Some specialize studies include subjects in the field of music and sports. There are also boarding schools that are exclusive for boys and girls.

International Schools

There are lots of international schools in the country that offer various courses in English. A student can receive a diploma or certificate upon completion which they could use if they wish to continue their studies in a college or university.

Parochial Schools

You can also enroll your child/ children in various Catholic and Protestant private schools that offer standard German education.

Home Schooling

Home – schooling is illegal in Germany. As per the law, it requires the students to attend legit private or public schools regardless if they are a German national or not.

Higher Education

There are many top colleges and universities in Germany which students attend for around 6 years. The classical universities provide a general education as part of the tradition of Alexander von Humboldt though in the past few years; there have been changes to the curriculum which allows a college student to get a Bachelor Degree after completing 4 years of study. There are technical universities in Germany that are more aimed at training students for specialized skills and/ or specific careers. It will also take about 4 years to complete. There are also schools that focuses on the studying the fields of art and music.

Entrance Requirements

When you're applying for entry into a German college or university, you must meet the following general requirements:

- **German Student Visa (VisumzuStudienzwecken):** This is not required if you are a citizen of an EU –

country. If you are a national of the following countries, you are required to get a student visa:

- o Canada
- o United States
- o Australia
- o Israel
- o Norway
- o Honduras
- o Switzerland
- o Iceland
- o Japan
- o San Marino
- o New Zealand
- o Monaco
- o Liechtenstein

- **Residence Permit:** This is required for non – EU applicants. There is a category specifically for expats who intends to study in Germany, or those who wanted to continue their studies in higher education. The application for this type of residence permit must be made within 3 months of your arrival in the country. Those who are EU nationals doesn't require such permit but they still need to register with the residents' registration authority similar to German nationals. Check out this website for more info: <www. aad.de/deutschland/in-deutschland/regeln/en/9143-reporting-to-the-authorities>

- **Entrance Qualification:** This is required for any student who wants to study or continue studying at a German university. For EU nationals, the school leaving certificate are recognized in Germany but for other foreign nationals outside the European Union, the school leaving certificates still needs to be evaluated. If the certificate is not deemed equivalent, then the student needs to take an assessment test. EU nationals must submit their applications at this website: www.hochschulstart.de while other foreign nationals should submit their applications directly to their chosen university.

- **Proficiency of German language:** Regardless if you're an EU national or not, you must be able to demonstrate your proficiency of the German language otherwise you could not be admitted to any higher education institution in the country except for International Degree Programs since it's being taught in English. It's ideal for expats to acquire a German Language Proficiency Certificate either in Germany or in your home country.

Chapter Eight: Taxes & Banking in Germany

Expats residing in the country are subjected to German taxes. This is true for foreign nationals who are earning an income from a German employer. The structure of the tax system in Germany has some similarities with other western and European countries. An individual needs to pay income taxes throughout the whole year, and it's usually being deducted from every pay check via the employer. Adjustments are made at the end of each year if there are any under/ overpayments of taxes.

Expats living in Germany for more than 90 days or for good will definitely need a German bank account. Setting up an account is simple if you will comply with all the needed requirements. Banks/ banking system in Germany pretty much operates the same way as in other banks around the world but with just a few twists. This chapter will give you an overview of the taxation and banking system in Germany.

Individual Income Taxes

Germany allows tax deductions to lower taxable income just like in its neighboring countries. Tax deductions are usually granted for specific cases such as minor children (under 18 years old), individuals under 27 years old that are still studying and doesn't have any source of income, specific insurance premiums, unavoidable expenses above a certain limit (due to illnesses etc.), and political/ charitable donations to German entities.

Deductions from compensations are created for 4 social programs:

- Retirement
- Health Insurance
- Unemployment
- Long – term Nursing Care

Payments for the aforementioned programs are equally paid by the employer and employee. The employer's share of taxes is not considered as a taxable income to the employee. The employee's share of taxable income also depends on a certain limit. Since most individuals are subject to tax this means that most income sources are taxable. The Wage Tax (Lohnsteuer) that accounts for 1/3 of the government's revenue is drawn from the employee's compensation.

If you are a self – employed individual, or you have other sources of income aside from your employer such as rent collections, fees from sidelines, investments etc. these are all covered via income tax (Einkommensteuer).

The only difference of the Wage Tax and the Income Tax is the method of tax collection. The Wage Tax is collected at source and it is directly paid to the tax office since it will automatically be deducted from an employee's salary therefore it is already care of one's employer. On the other hand, the Income Tax should be filed and paid the by the individual himself.

The tax office will estimate your tax for the current year based on your payment the previous year. The tax office will then require you to make pre – payments every quarter, or on the following dates:

- March 10
- June 10
- September 10
- December 10

The total tax that you're liable is determined by the income tax return that you file since this includes all types of income from other possible sources. Wage tax and provisional payments are deducted from the total tax liability so that a final tax payment or possible refund is properly assessed. The tax office issues a tax assessment between 2 and 6 months from the date in which the taxpayer filed his/ her tax returns. No payment will be due until an individual receives a tax assessment notice.

No payment will be due before receipts of the tax assessment notice. Keep in mind that every tax return will be audited which means that once an assessment is issued, it can only be change through extraordinary circumstances like tax evasion.

As a rule, the income tax return must be filed by May 31 of the year following the one wherein the income was received. If you seek assistance from a tax consultant, you can automatically have an extension to file until December 31, and in some cases it can even be extended until February

28 though there would be interests and penalties that you need to pay if you do not file your tax returns on time.

There are also some cases where a taxpayer is still required to pay taxes even if the income is less than the personal allowance especially in cases of tax – exempted income such as foreign – sourced income; there will still be an applicable income tax rate.

Other Taxes

In addition to different income taxes, there's also a variety of sales taxes that can impact both businesses and individuals in Germany. The Value Added Tax (Mehrwertsteuer) comes next to income taxes, and it also accounts for a quarter of the government's revenue. The VAT applies to goods and services in the country, and at the time of this writing, the current VAT rate is 19%. A reduced rate of 7% applies only to certain food products, and printed material. Insurance and medical services are exempted including exports of services rendered in other countries as well as goods abroad.

German Tax Classes

Employees are usually assigned under a various categories or certain Tax Class (Lohnsteuerklasse or Steuerklassen). Determining one's tax class is important because this is where the amount of withholding income tax deduction will be based. The tax class will also determine the amount of a taxpayer's social benefits, and the value of which an individual is eligible. A tax class may be assigned to an employee by tax authorities based on different criteria such as marital status, job/s etc. There could be instances where a taxpayer can request to be placed in a certain tax class.

Class I

This applies to the following individuals:

- Unmarried/ single individuals

- Registered Civil Partnership

- Divorced, Widowed, or Married unless they fall under the tax class II, III, or IV

Class II

Single Parents: Those who live alone with their child/ children are entitled to a child allowance as well as government assistance.

Class III

This applies to the following individuals:

- Married employees: if both spouses reside in Germany, and only one of them is a wage earner; or the other spouse earns an income but chooses to be categorized under the Class V.

- Widowed Employees: applies to the calendar year following the death of the husband/ wife if both are wage earners, and resides together in the country on the day the spouse died.

Class IV

This applies to married workers who live together in Germany but haven't selected to be categorized under tax Class III or V.

Class V

This is applicable if one of the spouses is categorized under Class III.

Class VI

This is an optional class for taxpayers who have more than one job or those who earn from other sources of income/ multiple jobs.

Tax Returns for U.S. Citizens

For American expats residing in Germany, you're likely aware of your expat tax filing requirements and you most probably know your obligation once the deadline every month of June approaches. However, recently, there's been some changes to the Foreign Bank Account Report deadline, and wherever you're residing, you will be affected by this big change. Here's what you should know about the upcoming changes regarding the tax deadline for U.S. citizens/ immigrants.

The tax deadline for American expatriates usually falls every 15th of June. Any Americans residing on tax day receives an automatic 2 – month extension. Keep in mind that you can also file an additional extension request which means that you could pay your expat taxes around the month of October. However, you should know that any taxes owed are supposed to be paid on tax day which means that you are responsible for paying interest (due to extensions) on any amount you owed until the IRS receives your payment. If you don't know how much you owe the U.S. government, you can check out the Form 1040 – ES so that you'll have an idea as to how much you need to pay.

State Taxes

This is not applicable to all American expats but if you came from certain states prior to your relocation, you may need to also file a state tax return aside from your expat taxes. You have to check the requirements in the state where you lived before making the move to know if you need to file state taxes. Some states follow the Federal filing deadline every 18th of April but most states follow their own deadlines. Be aware of such obligations so that you wouldn't miss the due dates.

General Requirements

If you haven't started preparing the filing of your expat taxes yet, then you better get that done as soon as you settle in your new home. One of the first things you need to do is to start compiling all the important paperwork including other tax information since you'll need these details whether you're going to hire a tax professional to do the work for you, or if you're going to file taxes on your own.

Understanding FATCA as an American Living in Germany

As an American expat, you are probably aware of just how confusing and tedious it is to file expat taxes. You will most likely need to take care of the additional reporting requirements that is specific to your tax situation like reporting your foreign financial accounts provided that you meet the filing threshold. One of the most common additional requirements for expats is the FATCA or Foreign Account Tax Compliance Act which came into effect in 2010.

Due to the FATCA, expats are now required to report their foreign bank account information to the IRS using the

Form 8938 should the accounts exceed a certain amount. Even if the FATCA form is quite new, it's quite similar to the information required by the Foreign Bank Account Report which is the reporting of foreign assets. Aside from filing Form 8938, the foreign financial institution of the American expat is also required to report the accounts to the IRS. The main purpose of FATCA is to make it easier for the American government to track its citizens and businesses that are earning either from their investments, or deposits in foreign financial accounts.

All American citizens must report their foreign assets to the IRS especially if they exceed specific thresholds while the foreign financial institution is required to report on the assets of their U.S. customers so that they won't have to pay 30% withholding on certain payments.

What Do I Need to Report?

These are the foreign assets and foreign bank accounts you need to report and include in your FATCA:

- Foreign pensions
- Foreign stockholdings
- Foreign partnership interests
- Foreign financial accounts
- Foreign mutual funds
- Foreign issued life insurance
- Foreign hedge funds
- Foreign real estate – it's not necessary for you to report the real estate but the foreign entity itself is a specified foreign financial asset, and its maximum value definitely includes the value of your estate.

Here's the breakdown of the filing threshold for U.S. citizens depending on one's status:

- **Single taxpayers residing abroad:** $200,000 on the last day of the tax year or $300,000 at any point during the year

- **Married taxpayers jointly living abroad:**

  $400,000 on the last day of the tax year or $600,000 at any point during the year

Additional Reporting Requirements

In setting up a foreign financial account, the financial institution will ask their expat clients to fill up a W – 9 forms. This kind of form is straightforward and simple, and its purpose is to provide your foreign bank with your tax information so that your bank can then file your income/ accounts to the IRS. Your foreign bank needs this W – 9 forms for informational purpose but it's not turned over to the IRS. If you are an American citizen, a U.S. Green Card holder, or your tax residence is in America, it's a requirement for you to complete the W – 9 form and submit it to your German bank or financial institution because if you don't, your foreign bank can withhold tax from your income or suspend your account so make sure to comply and submit on time.

It can be challenging for an American expat to determine what certain reporting requirements needs to be filed so make sure to take care of these even before you relocate to Germany. It's highly recommended that you seek the assistance of a tax professional so that you'll know your obligations, and the requirements that needs to be filed, or the process of how to file your U.S. taxes.

Banks and Banking in Germany

For expats, the general requirements to open a basic bank account are a passport, German address, and initial deposit. If you bring cash for your initial deposit along with the general requirements, then almost always you will be able to open a bank account immediately. On the other hand, if you will need to transfer funds from your home bank, it could take some time before the amount can be credited to your German bank account.

Giroaccount is the basic bank account of most Germans. It's quite similar to a current or checking account. Many banks in the country offer various services for bank fees with a Giroaccount. If you're a student, you can apply to be exempted from such bank fees. There are also savings accounts that usually offer better interest rates.

The EC Card

After you successfully opened a bank account, your bank will issue you an EC Card or locally known as an EC – Karte. This serves as your debit card that's connected to your bank account which you can use for daily transactions such as payments at gas stations, retail outlets, supermarkets, department stores, ticket offices and the likes. You can use your EC Card to also get cold cash from ATM machines (Geldautomat).

Payment is made via entering your 4 – digit PIN number, or your signature. In addition to the magnetic strip, your card should also have a chip. The chip can be used as a cash card, and you can load it for up to €200. You can also use it to pay for mini transactions like parking garages, and smaller outlets. Your EC Card can also be used if you need to get account statements or check your balance in ATM machines or special terminals of other banks.

Credit Cards

Credit cards are not widely popular in Germany since the Germans don't like the idea of having debt, but in recent years, it's becoming more and more accepted. There are now many international ATMs (Geldautomat) that will accept them for cash advances, and it can also be used in various transactions in hotels, restaurants, boutiques, malls, train tickets and the likes (although you need to check first if they

accept credit cards because some shops/ restaurants don't).
Credit cards can now also be used in telecom stores if you
need to purchase electronic equipment, or whenever you're
going to register for a mobile/ internet plans.

Online Banking

German banks have now embraced online banking; if
you register your account online, you can check your
balance, or transfer funds using your mobile phones or
computer. PIN numbers, passwords and user name are
issued to access your bank account online. TAN numbers
used in creating online transfers will be sent to the account
holder through SMS/ mobile, or via scanning a bar code
using a computer/ device.

Automatic Teller Machines (Geldautomat)

Geldautomat or ATMs are found in just about every
banks and major locations in Germany like train stations,
department stores, supermarkets, commercial areas, and

streets. You can easily recognize one because it has a large EC sign.

The ATMs can enable the holder to get cash not just in Germany but also in other neighboring European countries. If you use your EC card with the ATM machine of your bank, then almost always the transaction is free whereas if you do transactions using an international card or via an ATM that's a different bank than your own, you will need to pay for the charges especially if you do a withdrawal. Usually, the extra fees are a percentage of the amount withdrawn, though there are banks that charge a flat fee. The extra charge could cost around €1.00 to €10.00 depending on the bank, or the transaction. You can see if the ATM is an affiliated bank on the screen, or on the machine itself. Aside from checking your balance, and withdrawing cash from ATMs, you can also deposit or add funds to the chip of your EC card as well as put credits to your prepaid mobile phone.

Types of Banks

There are 4 types of banks in Germany, these are the following:

- Public sector commercial banks (Private Geschäftsbanken)
- Savings banks (Sparkassen)
- Credit cooperatives (Kreditgenossenschaften)
- Postbank

The distinctions between each of these aren't important for most account holders since the rules for creating a standard check or savings account is generally similar.

Payment Methods

Here are several ways of making payments in Germany:

Transfer *(Überweisung)*

From the name itself, you can transfer funds from one account to another. You just need to fill up a transfer form and personally submit it to your bank, or you can fill the form online, and just use a TAN number to finish your transaction.

Standing Order (Dauerauftrag)

This is usually how Germans pay their recurring payments like internet fees, insurance premiums, cable subscriptions, rent etc. The cost is automatically deducted from your bank account on a particular date that you set, and it is automatically transferred to the account of the recipient. You can fill out the necessary forms at your bank or via online. This is very convenient because you don't need to make individual payment for your recurring transactions; you just need to make sure that you have enough funds in your account to complete the payment process.

Direct debit (Lastschrift)

This is another practical method you can use to pay for your recurring transactions if it varies in size. You can give the recipient a direct debit authorization which means that they are authorize to deduct the respective amounts from your bank account. You can always cancel such authorization anytime if you feel like the recipient is getting more than what needs to be paid. As a safeguard against such misdemeanors, you have the control to recall any sum that was deducted in this manner for 90 days. You have an unrestricted right to recall it even if it's properly done though of course you will have an unpaid bill.

Other Bank Services

Other bank services include Dispositionskredit wherein an account holder can establish a line of credit at a German bank (2 – 3 times your monthly pay). Once the account holder completed this, he/ she can overdraw the account to the agreed amount though such overdrafts can cost the holder to huge interests every year (around 11% to 18%).

In contrast with Anglo – American banks, German banks offer their holders with wider range of financial/ banking services that goes beyond deposits and lending. You can purchase stocks, bonds and insurance, you can exchange currencies, get traveller's checks, buy properties, make electronic transfers worldwide, set up an online portfolio/ asset management account, buy metals, and get mortgages for your dream house. There are also many banks in Germany that has International Desks which are designed to aid expats, and English – speaking foreigners regarding their banking/ financial needs while in Germany. International Desks can also help expats in getting information about various financial products and banking services being offered by the banks.

German banks are open from Monday thru Fridays at 8:30 AM to 4 PM; on Thursdays though, some of them extend until 6:30 PM. Smaller branches are closed during lunchtime but you can use the ATMs of most banks 24/7.

Chapter Nine: Healthcare and Retirement in Germany

Germany is widely known for having one of the world – class health care systems, providing its citizens/ residents with quality health insurance coverage. Around 85% of residents in Germany is part of the voluntary membership of the country's health care scheme while the rest have health insurance coverage from private insurance companies. In 2007 the German government required all of its residents including expatriates residing in the country to be insured for a hospital and an out – patient medical treatment as well as medical check – ups and pregnancy. This chapter will cover the public health insurance system in Germany as well as the private sector.

Public Insurance System

Government Health Insurance System (GKV)

As mentioned earlier majority of German residents (around 70 million) are members of the public healthcare system. For instance, if your gross salary is below €59,400 per year, or around €4,900 per month you are then required to avail the GKV healthcare scheme. The GKV has a basic rate of 14.6% including a median supplemental rate of 1% from your eligible gross income to a maximum monthly income of around €4,400. If you earn a larger gross income, you are not required to pay a higher insurance cost.

Assuming that an employee's maximum monthly premium is around €700, your contribution is around €377 while your employer will pay around €323. The minimum period of membership with a GKV is 18 months. You can also choose to switch to government health fund providers but you need to at least give a 2 month notice after the 18 month membership, or if a supplemental insurance premium is either increased or demanded.

The medical benefits included in hospital care are as a ward patient with a physician on duty at your nearest hospital as well as out – patient care with registered physicians and basic dental care.

Do take note that coverage is not included if you're going to get a private physician or surgeons, private room, homeopathic medical care, vision products, dental subsidies, or any medical benefits outside the European continent. You non – working depends residing at your address in the country are covered at no additional cost but they still need to be properly registered with the same GKV as the paying member.

If you want to join the German government system, you can register at any of the 113 GKVs which are non – profit organizations administrating the health scheme of the government. This doesn't mean that the health benefits are different since all health insurance funds must follow the government regulation on the minimum benefits they offer. The premiums may only vary if there'll be new regulations. It's highly recommended that you research which voluntary supplemental programs are best so that you can avail no – claims bonus, discounted or free check – ups, or discount in health travel plans.

Important Tip:

It's probably best that you ask the possibility of the staff explaining the policies to you in English so that you can fully understand it because it could be difficult to understand if you're not yet that proficient with the German language though there are only a few that offers such service or has an English speaking staff.

Keep in mind that you and your dependents should also be a member of the government's long – term nursing care scheme because this will cover the cost of personal nursing needs like bathing, feeding, and overall caring in the event of disability. In 2017, a major reform of the nursing care was instituted and this is why the cost became a bit more expensive. The cost is anywhere between 2.50% and 2.80% of an employee's gross salary, at the time of this writing (Maximum of € 123/ month for those who have no children). This makes a total of around € 820 per month if you're earning €4,000 or more as an employee while your employer contributes around €380; this includes dependent spouses and children living in the country.

If you would like insurance coverage to supplement the government health insurance system, you can have a choice of buying an insurance policy from a private company (from a German company, or an international company) so that you would be able to reimburse the costs of a private physician, private room, homeopathy, and other alternative medical treatment, or other higher dental reimbursements.

Emergency evacuation from places outside the country that includes a private travel insurance policy must also be taken into consideration because these aren't paid for by the government health insurance policy, and it would be quite expensive to pay for benefits out of pocket.

Government health insurance funds sometimes include supplemental insurance plans from a private provider that offers group rebates. Such tied plans aren't always ideal since you have a wider choice of options from private health insurance companies.

Private Health Insurance (PKV)

Private health insurances cover various options for medical and dental treatments plus it reaches broader geographical locations. By acquiring a private health insurance you can avail more medical services and profession. Both hospitals and physicians depend to a certain extent on private patients to increase their earnings, which is why they welcome people who have private health insurance plans. A private patient can also get a doctor that can speak their native language which is why it's advisable for foreign expats. There are around 40 top – notch German companies that provide private health insurance, and there are various premium packages available to suit any type of budget. The cost per person depends on the medical policy one will avail, the chosen benefits, pre – existing medical conditions, and also the entry age. A major portion of your medical insurance premium is also included in the tax deductible of your income taxes.

The government insurance premium covers both you and your dependents whereas private medical insurance policies each member covered are paid for separately. You can reduce the monthly cost of your private insurance by agreeing to an excess or a deductible. Private health insurance companies in Germany aren't allowed to cancel an insurance policy if the holder submits claims and the company is also required to set aside 10% of your premiums aside as a provision so that the cost will be stable when you reach your retirement age.

If you're would like to buy an expatriate health insurance as an alternative for the government insurance policy, this could be quite tedious since most foreign insurance companies aren't registered with the BaFin. Even those companies who are members have health insurance policies that don't meet the standards set in the new reforms. This is because the German government doesn't want to set upper limits on reimbursement levels, and there shouldn't be out – of – pocket deductibles annually that are more than €5,000.

Try to avoid limited – term plans with no requirement for medical underwriting because such policies may not offer permanent extension, and don't cover pre – existing conditions. Should you decide to stay longer than the contractual term (around 1 to 5 years), and the contract of the health insurance expires, it could be more expensive and harder to acquire a new health coverage. Aside from that, even if you have purchased such a plan from a health insurance company in Germany, it may not be recognized by visa authorities once you arrive in the country, which means that you could be forced to get a permanent health insurance plan in order for you to have the permission to stay plus you may also pay penalties.

Retirement for Expats in Germany

Unfortunately, Germany is not a go – to place for expatriate retirees compared to other European countries like France or Spain; the main hindrance is the difficult process of acquiring a residency permit because unlike other countries, Germany doesn't offer a retirement visa or something similar.

However, if you are a retiree, and you still like to relocate to Germany but you're not a citizen of Switzerland, or other countries within the European Economic Area (EEA), you'll need to apply for a permit; either through marrying a German national/ permanent resident holder, or an investment visa though such categories may have age limitations.

Once you successfully acquired a visa through marriage or investment categories, you are required to wait for 3 years before finally getting a permanent resident permit. You can read more information regarding this matter by contacting your local German Embassy, or going to the official website of the Ministry of Interior at

https://www.bmi.bund.de

Retirement Contributions

All employees in the country are required to pay contributions to Germany's pension schemes. If you're a foreign national who works in the country, and plans to retire here, do take note that you will have to pay for pension contributions until you are 67 years old.

At the time of this writing, the contributions are generally calculated around 19% of an employee's gross salary off of a maximum salary of around €5,600 per month.

For instance, in 2013, the maximum monthly contribution is €1,096 payable as €548 by both the employer and employee. You don't need to pay more than what is required from the portion of your salary that exceeds the amount needed.

Health Care for Retirees

Health care is one of the "must – haves" for any retirees. The healthcare service in the country is quite similar to the National Health Service in Great Britain. If you're not a citizen of Switzerland, or other countries within the European Economic Area (EEA), you must have an adequate medical insurance to cover your health needs upon application for a resident permit.

If you're a citizen of EEA countries, and Switzerland make sure to get a valid European Health Insurance card before you apply for a resident permit because this insurance cared will enable you to get health services in the country at a discounted price or sometimes for free.

Majority of retirees like to maintain the pre – retirement standard of living. However, many people, particularly average income earners, know that their savings will not last for a long time due to inflation and long life expectancy rates. For instance, a data gathered by HSBC found out that a retirement plan in the UK only lasts for around 19 years on average; and major problems that can cause financial burdens emerge after 7 years which is why financial experts recommend that one should plan for retirement as early as possible and plan one's finances to cover any future expenses particularly health – related issues.

Chapter Ten: Getting Married in Germany

Marriages between two persons are deemed as legally binding contracts or legal unions. It is a tradition that has been protected from the outset under the government constitution of different countries. Any couple who wanted to get married in Germany should personally appear for a civil ceremony at a Standesamt. Unlike in other countries, civil wedding in Germany requires no presence of witnesses. The cost of the civil wedding including processing of documents can cost anywhere between €65 and €200.

Ceremonies are conducted using the national language which is why some foreign nationals who aren't proficient in German choose to have an interpreter during the rites. This chapter will cover the overview of the marriage process in Germany particularly for expatriates.

Marriage Requirements

First and foremost, if you and your partner (regardless if one is an expat, or both of you are) decide to get married in Germany, you must get the paperwork going as soon as possible since there will be lots of legal formalities that you need to attend to. Usually, couples prepare several months before their planned wedding day especially if you have certain issues such as previous marriages, resident permit problems etc.

One of the first things you need to do once you and your partner plan to marry in the country is to go to the local magistrate's office or perhaps in your local German embassy. These offices will give you information on what kind of documentation and requirements you need.

Requirements will vary from one region to another, and it will also depend on your previous marital status, nationality, and other issues related to you or your partner. Here are some general documents you will need:

- Valid passport
- Official birth certificate
- Proof of a minimum of 21 days of continuous residence in Germany
- Proof of being single
- Birth certificates of children (if any) the couple may have had together
- The required application and questionnaire from the Standesamt

Other requirements like Certificate of No Impediment (CNI), marriage certificates from previous marriages, and financial statements may also be required by the local magistrate's office.

People who were previously married must present proof of divorce papers, or death certificate. The former may cause some problems because usually a decree from a British or American court is not enough. One may need to prove that the decree can no longer be contested which is why it's necessary to get a statement from the court that granted the divorce.

Certified translations of non – German language will be required as well as other documents that shouldn't be older than 6 months.

If one or both partners is a foreigner

If either one of the partners is a foreign national, expect that the documents will be sent to a higher regional court for verification of status.

Those planning to return to their home country one day may wish to consider the legal status of their partner because there could be certain conditions that could keep the partner from living with you such as medical condition, nationality, or criminal record. Just visit your local embassy regarding on all emigration formalities. It's also best to know if your marriage in Germany will be recognized in your homeland.

Civil and Traditional Ceremonies

Civil weddings in Germany avoid any sort of trappings that could be rightly or wrongly deemed as too religious. Some Jews, Christians, Muslims, and even atheists get married at the registrar's office which is why the interior is as neutral as possible become some can be quite sensitive especially when it comes to their faith. Nevertheless, you will find the wedding rooms to be great especially if the space is filled with a wedding atmosphere like flowers, deep carpeting, subdued lighting and the likes. In some states in Germany, the magistrate's office has sort of a classy feel to it depending on the location of the district.

After a civil ceremony, most couples would still want to have a traditional wedding; fortunately, the country has many magnificent palaces, cathedrals, and even castles that offer wedding arrangements.

Same - Sex Marriage

Civil Partnerships Law is legally recognized in the country since 2001. The passing of this law pave the way for same – sex marriage in Germany. The process is pretty much the same when entering into a civil marriage, and at the time there were still some legal differences. In 2017, the German legislature removed such legal differences, and on October 1 of the same year, same – sex marriage was legally approved including all the obligations and benefits that are prescribed by the German Constitution.

Relocation Tips

You and your family will need to do careful planning before, and after you moved out of your home country, and moved into your new home in Germany. Your relocation plan will highly depend on your own living situations but key factors such as your status, age, purpose, and financial capacity will definitely influence the complexity of your relocation. Those who are young, single, and working individuals will have a less complicated situation when it comes to moving into another country compared to those who will move with their families and those expat retirees who may need someone to look after them.

This chapter will focus on all the most important things you need to consider ahead of your move. This is a practical checklist for you and your family so that you'll know what to do, and will have enough time to take care of your unique situations, and so that you won't miss out anything. There are many aspects when relocating to a foreign country; this pre – moving checklist will guide you at the different planning stage of your relocation including how to legally move to Germany with your family as well as your possessions.

A Few Weeks Before Relocation

Here's a breakdown of all the items that needs to be organized weeks prior to your departure date:

- Everything that needs to be sold or donated must already be done; your freezer, cellar, food storage must already be emptied out. All the items you're going to leave behind should either be gone or put into storage. Your other pending items like laundry should already be picked up; your plants should be taken care of or given away to neighbors. It's also best to stay with your nearby relatives, friends or hotel if you're bed is already packed up.

- Make sure that you and your family are already packed up; this includes the things you'll bring to the airport with you, and the luggage containing your personal items. Make sure that you have enough clothes once you arrive in Germany while you're waiting for your other stuff to be shipped.

The Day of Moving

- You should already be either out of the house (especially if you hired a professional cleaning service so that they'll have time to clean it) or in a hotel or nearby friend so you can have time to relax as well.

- Take one last final meter readings of your electricity, water, gas or telephone. Unplug or close all the circuits before you leave.

- After everything is moved out, check the property one last time, and well, say your goodbyes.

- You need to make sure that all your travel documents, visas, permits etc. are ready and can be easily access to avoid any hassles.

PHOTO REFERENCES

Page 1 Photo by werner22brigitte via Pixabay.com,

https://pixabay.com/en/brandenburger-tor-dusk-dawn-201939/

Page 4 Photo by Analogicus via Pixabay.com,

https://pixabay.com/en/koblenz-german-corner-sachsen-3453860/

Page 7 Photo by FelixMittermeir via Pixabay.com,

https://pixabay.com/en/bundestag-german-flag-reichstag-2463236/

Page 14 Photo by geralt via Pixabay.com,

https://pixabay.com/en/freiburg-city-germany-road-houses-76217/

Page 15 Photo by Tilgner Pictures via Pixabay.com,

https://pixabay.com/en/berlin-spree-river-architecture-2168118/

Page 17 Photo by Jollymama via Pixabay.com,

https://pixabay.com/en/bavaria-germany-allg%C3%A4u-costume-205730/

Page 18 Photo by 089photoshootings via Pixabay.com,

https://pixabay.com/en/man-bavaria-dirndl-folklore-woman-1979269/

Page 19 Photo by Tama66 via Pixabay.com,

https://pixabay.com/en/city-houses-small-town-architecture-3378773/

Page 20 Photo by TrepTowerAlex via Pixabay.com,

https://pixabay.com/en/germany-3672754/

Page 22 Photo by tknight67 via Pixabay.com,

https://pixabay.com/en/bratwurst-europe-food-sauerkraut-1446708/

Page 23 Photo by Marco Verch via Flickr.com,

https://www.flickr.com/photos/149561324@N03/43075520502/in/photolist

Page 24 Photo by WordRidden via Flickr.com,

https://www.flickr.com/photos/wordridden/8022821879/in/p
hotolist

Page 25 Photo by Marco Verch via Flickr.com,

ttps://www.flickr.com/photos/149561324@N03/35700065104/i
n/photolist

Page 26 Photo by 12019 via Pixabay.com,

https://pixabay.com/en/germany-mountains-fog-autumn-
fall-1828011/

Page 30 Photo by MaxxMcGee via Pixabay.com,

https://pixabay.com/en/folk-music-customs-group-of-
people-1871094/

Page 37 Photo by Ivabalk via Pixabay.com,

https://pixabay.com/en/kurort-rathen-port-ship-ferry-
3529660/

Page 39 Photo by Noelsch via Pixabay.com,

https://pixabay.com/en/passport-document-germany-
249420/

Page 58 Photo by Guentherlig via Pixabay.com,

https://pixabay.com/en/hamburg-speicherstadt-channel-2976711/

Page 60 Photo by Melancholia Photography via Pixabay.com,

https://pixabay.com/en/berlin-tv-tower-nikolaiviertel-dom-1467502/

Page 62 Photo by Lapping via Pixabay.com,

https://pixabay.com/en/frankfurt-maximum-hesse-germany-1827520/

Page 63 Photo by 12019 via Pixabay.com,

https://pixabay.com/en/munich-germany-city-cities-urban-391354/

Page 64 Photo by scholacantorum via Pixabay.com,

https://pixabay.com/en/leipzig-outlook-panorama-city-3704342/

Page 65 Photo by Wolfgang_Vogt via Pixabay.com,

https://pixabay.com/en/stuttgart-new-castle-schlo%C3%9Fplatz-2109990/

Page 66 Photo by Taxi Cologne via Pixabay.com,

https://pixabay.com/en/dom-cologne-cathedral-cologne-2092871/

Page 67 Photo by Moerschy via Pixabay.com,

https://pixabay.com/en/hamburg-port-elbe-landungsbr%C3%BCcken-832421/

Page 68 Photo by Skeeze via Pixabay.com,

https://pixabay.com/en/windmill-lake-park-trees-landscape-1606642/

Page 69 Photo by EvgeniT via Pixabay.com,

https://pixabay.com/en/dortmund-night-light-b236-3356819/

Page 70 Photo by Andrea Mettallerreni via Pixabay.com,

https://pixabay.com/en/castle-dresden-city-germany-54758/

Page 72 Photo by Andy Leung HK via Pixabay.com,

https://pixabay.com/en/dresden-tram-germany-city-european-2669877/

Page 76 Photo by Gellinger via Pixabay.com,

https://pixabay.com/en/christmas-market-nuremberg-550345/

Page 82 Photo by HPGruesen via Pixabay.com,

https://pixabay.com/en/truss-historically-stolberg-resin-1731118/

Page 93 Photo by FBHK via Pixabay.com,

https://pixabay.com/en/village-landscape-houses-1784455/

Page 110 Photo by geralt via Pixabay.com,

https://pixabay.com/en/success-curve-arrow-turn-on-2917048/

Page 116 Photo by fancycrave1 via Pixabay.com,

https://pixabay.com/en/ipad-tablet-technology-touch-820272/

Page 124 Photo by HendoBe via Pixabay.com,

https://pixabay.com/en/frankfurt-city-1739362/

Page 139 Photo by Guenther Dillingen via Pixabay.com,

https://pixabay.com/en/road-city-tourism-architecture-3161962/

Page 147 Photo by ernestoeslava via Pixabay.com,

https://pixabay.com/en/education-people-school-child-3189934/

Page 161 Photo by Image4You via Pixabay.com,

https://pixabay.com/en/euro-coins-currency-money-yellow-1353420/

Page 176 Photo by Bru-no via Pixabay.com,

https://pixabay.com/en/skyline-skyscraper-city-bridge-3582111/

Page 186 Photo by Roger Blackwell via Flickr.com,

https://www.flickr.com/photos/rogerblackwell/25636613331/

Page 196 Photo by SalFalko via Flickr.com,

https://www.flickr.com/photos/safari_vacation/7348085308/

Page 198 Photo by Reuben Straver via Flickr.com,

https://www.flickr.com/photos/cutey5/14620420877/in/photolist

Page 205 Photo by Dar1930 via Pixabay.com,

https://pixabay.com/en/illuminated-evening-winter-1479168/

REFERENCES

Living in Germany – Germany – Visa.org

https://www.germany-visa.org/living-in-germany/

Expat "How To" Guides for Germany - German-Way.com

https://www.german-way.com/for-expats/living-in-germany/expat-how-to-guides-for-germany/

Moving to Germany: Guide to German visas and permits - Expatica.com

https://www.expatica.com/de/visas-and-permits/Moving-to-Germany-Guide-to-German-visas-and-permits_102738.html

Work in Germany: Finding a job in Germany - Expatica.com

https://www.expatica.com/de/employment/Work-in-Germany-Jobs-in-Germany_102718.html

How To Open a Bank Account in Germany - German-Way.com

https://www.german-way.com/for-expats/living-in-germany/expat-how-to-guides-for-germany/how-to-open-a-bank-account-in-germany/

Germany - Climate and Weather - Expatfocus.com

http://www.expatfocus.com/expatriate-germany-climate-weather

Buying a House or Apartment in Germany - Howtogermany.com

https://www.howtogermany.com/pages/housebuying.html

Guide To Germany - Etiquette, Customs, Culture & Business - Kwintessential.co.uk

https://www.kwintessential.co.uk/resources/guides/guide-to-germany-etiquette-customs-culture-business/

What is the Average Cost of Living in Germany - Liveworkgermany.com

https://liveworkgermany.com/2017/03/what-is-the-average-cost-of-living-in-germany/

Cost of Living in Germany - Numbeo.com

https://www.numbeo.com/cost-of-living/country_result.jsp?country=Germany

Internet in Germany - Settle-in-berlin.com

https://www.settle-in-berlin.com/internet-in-germany-providers/

Retirement for Expats in Germany - Expatbriefing.com

https://www.expatbriefing.com/country/germany/living/retirement-for-expats-in-germany.html

What Does It Cost to Study in Germany - Studying-in-germany.org

https://www.studying-in-germany.org/what-does-it-cost-to-study-in-germany/

Health Insurance Options in Germany - Howtogermany.com/

https://www.howtogermany.com/pages/healtinsurance2.html

www.ingramcontent.com/pod-product-compliance
Lightning Source LLC
Chambersburg PA
CBHW071422090426
42737CB00011B/1544